Funny Shit
in the Woods

And Other Stories

—

The Best of Semi-Rad.com

by Brendan Leonard

To anyone who's ever shared a Semi-Rad.com post with someone else

CONTENTS

Introduction   1

1   The Rules For Dating A Dirtbag   7

2   How To Shit In The Woods, And How Not To   11

3   The Ineloquence Of Talking About The Outdoors   17

4   How To Get Your New Boyfriend/Girlfriend To Hate Your Sport   21

5   How To Talk Shit To Your Climbing Partner   25

6   7 Tips On How To Be A Good Tentmate   31

7   Beware The Urine-Drinking Mountain Goats   35

8   Are You Ready For Your Summit Photo?   39

9   Hey Coffee, I Love You   43

10 How To Bark Down A Dog   47

11 Advanced Techniques For The Well-Rounded Climber   51

12 Announcing A New Line Of Invisible Climbing Outerwear   55

13 Lose Weight Now With The 10,000-Foot Diet   59

14 The Greatest Mountaineering Survival Story Never Told   63

15 Are You A Beautiful And Unique Snowflake?   69

16 Do You Have Obsessive Campfire Adjustment Syndrome?   73

17 The Masochist's Guide To Bushwhacking   77

18 Big Shout-Out To Rocks   81

19 Don't Sandbag Me, Bro   85

20 You Don't Have To Clip That To The Outside Of Your Pack   89

21   Review: My Running Shoes   93

22   The Beer Gratitude Scale For Outdoorsfolk   97

23   The Cars Without That New-Car Smell   101

24   Dude, It's OK To Hug Your Bro   107

25   Hiking Is Cool   111

26   9 Reasons You Should Never Bike To Work   115

27   Make This Year The Year Of Maximum Enthusiasm   121

28   The Pure Joy Of Fixie Dave   127

29   The Guy Who Puts The Fun Back In Fun   131

30   Please Continue Instagramming Your Amazing Life   135

31   The Importance Of Being A Lifelong Beginner   139

32   Do You Have The Stoke?   143

33   The Importance Of Big Dreams   147

34   Why Road Trips Are Still Important   151

35   The Moments Before Your Big Moments   155

36   Your Best Vacation Is Someone's Worst Nightmare   159

37   Sometimes You Get A High-Five From The Universe   163

38   The Not-So-Bad Bad Day   167

39   How To Friend Someone In Real Life   171

40   Make Plans, Not Resolutions   175

INTRODUCTION

In February 2011, I paid $15 for the url www.semi-rad.com, hoping to build a blog and share some of my outdoor stories there. I picked up a cheap, and also very ugly, Wordpress theme, and the Twitter handle @semi_rad, and started typing some stories and essays in my downtime as I worked from home as a tech copywriter. I decided I would put up a new blog post every Thursday, to keep myself disciplined, and so people would know to regularly check back once a week (if they liked the writing enough to remember the name of the website).

That first month, Semi-Rad.com got about 600 page views. I thought that was pretty good—"people are reading my stuff!" I told myself. I kept at it. After a few months, Steve Casimiro from Adventure Journal contacted me and asked if he could re-run some of my blog posts on his website, and I of course said yes, thank you, that would be incredible exposure. I wrote a post about thanking your friends with beer when they did outdoor-related favors for you, like loaning you gear. Steve picked it up, and it went pretty viral on Adventure-Journal.com, with a few hundred Facebook "likes." Steve ran a few more posts of mine, and I started to gain traffic. A few people who read the "about" page on Semi-Rad seemed to identify with the ethos of "crushing it, kind of," and the mentality that you didn't have to climb 5.14 or make the podium to have a blast in the outdoors.

After I had stuck with it for almost a year, I gained enough momentum to rationalize making some stickers to build publicity for the site. My friend Josh Barker, who is a branding genius, designed the first sticker, and came up with the brilliant tagline "Happily Semi-Rad," which made the stickers—and the website—a "we" thing instead of a "me" thing. To me, it always has been a "we thing." When I sit down to come up with each week's post, I always ask, What will resonate with people?

Thankfully, some of the stories have resonated with people, and I've watched the social media shares grow along with the web traffic, and received e-mails and messages from awesome people reaching out to say thanks for writing this piece or that piece. Sometimes people need something to make them laugh, and sometimes they need something to make them think.

When you decide to become a writer, people tell you to never give away your stuff for free, that you're professional, and you should get paid for it. I did exactly the opposite with Semi-Rad, and gave away some of my best stuff for free. I wrote about 90 posts on Semi-Rad before I ever got a dollar for sponsorship or advertising on the site. Thankfully, a few sponsors have seen the value in it and stood behind the brand and kept me going for nearly four years (as of the publication of this book).

I put a giant Semi-Rad.com sticker on the side of my van in summer 2012, and a really cool thing started happening at trailheads and parking lots: People would come up and say hi because they were familiar with the website, or liked a particular story. I got to meet so many people that way, people I never would have had a reason to chat with if I hadn't had a giant sticker on my van.

There are a million different writers out there, and a million different ways to succeed as a writer: You can work to get published in the bigger, respectable magazines and journals, or collect awards, or write a bestselling book. Every week, you get to decide where to focus your creative energy.

Every week since February 2011, I've put my energy into the pieces I put on Semi-Rad.com, whether they're heartfelt, meditative, or just goofy. I've never won any awards, or gotten published in The New Yorker or a big-time (or small-time) literary journal. I'm excited to do it for the high-fives I get, through e-mail or in person.

This book is my way of collecting the best and most popular pieces from Semi-Rad.com and putting them together in a place where you don't have to scroll and click for hours to get a sense of what it's all about. If Semi-Rad has reached you on any level over the past four years, I hope this book gives you a way to carry some of that humor and stoke around with you— maybe even up in the mountains or on a river trip—or, give a gift to someone who you think would enjoy it. Thanks for reading.

-Brendan Leonard
Denver, Colorado
October 2014

PART 1:

SOME FUNNY SHIT

1

THE RULES FOR DATING A DIRTBAG

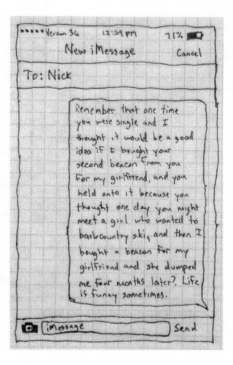

It's a singular feeling when you're 33 and talking to your mother and she says, "You know what I think you should try? Match.com."

Then there's another feeling when you say to your mother, "Well, Mom, I had this weird feeling about meeting women and telling them I live in a van full of climbing gear, but then I realized I really only am interested in women who could be interested in a guy who lives in a van full of climbing gear. If that makes any sense." I think my mom is really proud.

There are some interesting things about dating people who love the outdoors, aren't there? Like you fantasize about dating someone who loves to go backpacking, and then you find out that it's really hard to spoon when you're each zipped up in a sleeping bag and it's too cold to put your arms outside of it. And even though you think it would be rad to have a significant other who climbs, you go on a climbing date and are sure your partner/potential girlfriend or boyfriend has lost all respect for you when you get Elvis leg and start whining as you freak out on the crux move a few feet off the belay. Or you want them to live their dreams and you want to live your dreams, but it kind of sucks when they're gone leading a wilderness trip for a month, or you're gone for a two-month bike tour and you have to get out your phone and look at photos of them to remember what they look like.

But then of course, you get all those sunsets and sunrises together, and maybe you get to hold hands during that last wide part of the trail walking to the car, and instead of sitting on a rock somewhere looking over an alpine lake wondering about girls, you get to sit on that same rock with a girl and talk to her about hip hop and books and what she was like in high school and all that.

But is it unromantic to buy your girlfriend an avalanche beacon for Valentine's Day? Because I did that once, and what I thought it said was, "Here's something that means we can spend time together in the backcountry." But I could definitely see someone taking it the wrong way, especially because it came with a shovel.

I mean, I want to open doors for a girl. Give you my jacket when we go to a movie and you're cold walking home. Cook you breakfast when you're sleeping in on a Saturday. But it begins to get fuzzy at the trailhead. Although I'm a gentleman and you're a lady, you will be carrying either the rope, or the rack. Take the tent, or the stove and fuel and pots. If I am cooking us dinner over a camp stove, you are setting up the tent, or vice versa. Right?

My friend Teresa went on a couple dates with this guy in Seattle, and thought it was going pretty well. The third date, she invited him over to barbecue, and they met at a grocery store to pick up a couple things before riding to her house. Which, at the time was at the top of 8th Avenue, a 30-block steadily uphill ride into a headwind. He had told her he did some cycling, and had finished a handful of races and road rides. So she was surprised when he stayed behind her for the entire ride up the hill. Into a headwind. The entire ride. "I mean, are you fucking kidding me?" she said when she re-told me the story a couple weeks ago. Either the guy didn't know anything about cycling etiquette and had lied about his experience, or he was a jerk. Either way, that was their last date.

My friend Sara told me last year she was done dating climbers, for a number of reasons—a lot of men she dated seemed to like the idea of being with someone who was a climber, but didn't like the reality; or she found

9

herself having more fun climbing with her girlfriends and platonic male friends than a romantic partner; or the dating pool was just too small if she limited herself to only climbers. Now she's happy with a guy whose main thing is paragliding, and he's remembering how to belay and they're climbing together and actually having fun doing it.

Teresa said one time, I just feel like men at the climbing gym are so focused on climbing that they don't notice women. I said Are you shitting me? Of course we do. At least I do. As a man, I will tell you there is nothing we are so focused on that we don't notice women. Nothing. We may be too dumb to notice when you are interested, but we never fail to notice. If I speak for other dudes who are dirtbags, we are especially in tune when we see a woman who exhibits characteristics that suggest she likes to wear backpacks, or sleep in the dirt, or do pullups.

Sometimes I say there is no better sound in the world than a beautiful woman laughing, except the sound of a beautiful woman laughing at something I said. But then I think the sound of a beautiful woman yelling "On belay!" from 120 feet above me is better. Especially if it's after she led the crux pitch on the route.

—

2

HOW TO SHIT IN THE WOODS,
AND HOW NOT TO

It was the night before my 5-day backpacking trip with five tough

teenagers from East Palo Alto when someone asked about toilet paper,

and we discovered we hadn't been issued any. This was most of the kids' first

time in any sort of backcountry outside the Bay Area, and each seemed to

have a different solution to the problem.

"I'm just gonna hold it for five days," Eric said. The kids all seemed to

know another guy who had gone on a similar backpacking trip, and legendarily "held it" until he got back to a proper commode with some soft, fluffy white tissue paper.

"I bet that thing came out with a fist on the end of it," I said. "You guys will just have to use rocks and sticks." This suggestion was met with denial, disbelief, and shock. Two minutes before, I was Friendly White Hippie Dude. Now the kids were looking at me like I was a creepy guy with a strange fetish they wished they didn't know about.

The first shit in the woods is a pure rite of passage for any mountain person. Sure, you can be a casual day hiker for years and avoid it, and maybe even last through a few overnight trips. But sooner or later, you'll need to confront your ancestral self and drop one amongst the evergreens, without your favorite magazine, scented candle, or plush bathroom rug under your toes.

Nowadays, we bury it under the ground when hiking in the backcountry. On raft trips, it goes in the Groover, an ammo can fitted with a toilet seat. On the side of El Capitan, it goes in bags and gets stuffed in a PVC pipe with two screw caps, the "poop tube," and hauled up the wall with the rest of the supplies. On some glaciers in Denali National Park, you go in a bear canister-esque Clean Mountain Can (try not to pee in it) that you carry out with you. On some boats and float houses, it's heated in an incinerating toilet until it turns into ash (about 1200 degrees Fahrenheit), and then it's dumped in the ocean. On Mount Shasta, the Forest Service issues poop bags complete with paper targets for aiming, and after the magic happens, you pick up the target, roll it up and bag it, and carry it down the mountain. In the Grand Canyon, mules carry it out after a couple of dudes in HazMat suits shovel it out of the pit toilets at Indian Gardens.

In the 1979 Book of Strange Facts and Useless Information, author Scot Morris writes: "Australian aborigines, who usually go naked and are unconcerned if a stranger sees them defecating, are deeply ashamed to be seen eating." Our society is far from comfortable with it, requiring complete privacy, flushing the evidence out of sight as soon as possible, and covering our tracks with fans, sprays and matches. Some teenage boys maintain that women don't do it at all. Parents of newborn babies will change an average of 2,800 "dirty diapers" in the baby's first year, but we panic at the thought of having to squat in the forest. And we can't imagine wiping our ass with anything other than toilet paper.

But it's not so bad. A breeze blowing through the Ponderosa pines, maybe the noise of a creek trickling by at the speed of nature, and no constipated ad salesman grunting one out in the next stall, farts echoing off the inside of the toilet, squealing like angry ducks. We can take our time. Get away from the trail as far as you need to feel comfortable—at least 100 feet. Dig a hole at least 6 inches deep (this can sometimes be aided considerably if you can find a large rock embedded in soil, and you can pry it out, leaving a large hole). Pull your pants down to your ankles, line yourself up over the hole, squat, hug your knees and relax. Poop like the perfectly normal human you were 300 years ago, before we got all soft and had to drink bottled water and have someone else kill our food.

Some folks pack a roll of Charmin Ultra Soft, but I can't bear to pack it out once it's used. Some of us choose to use rocks, sticks or leaves, which have the advantages of a) leaving nothing to pack out and b) an unlimited supply of wiping material. The two criteria to keep in mind when hunting for potential rocks and sticks are a) smoothness and b) ability to fit the rock or stick between your butt cheeks. The best, of course, is a summer snowbank in the mountains, which provide infinite refreshing snowballs. When you're finished, bury your rocks and sticks in the hole, and off you go down the trail.

You miss the comforts of civilized shitting when you're in the backcountry, but also the discomforts. No filthy toilet seats, no public restroom doors that don't lock, no senators from Idaho propositioning you with foot Morse code from the next stall, and no lines. Few things can go wrong in the woods, usually.

But things can, in fact, go horribly wrong. On Mount Rainier once, as the story goes as told to me by a friend who heard the story from a guide who at that time worked for Rainier Mountaineering Inc., a client left his team and guides to go take a dump. On Rainier, of course, climbers are required to "blue bag" it and pack it out with them (or toss it in one of the receptacles on the mountain, which are removed by helicopter once a year). Most folks unclip the leg loops of their harness, pull their pants down, plop one in the snow and pick it up with the blue bag, as you would do with your dog's poop in a municipal park.

After a few minutes, the Rainier climber returned to the group, frantically repeating to the guide, "I can't find my shit!" In the ensuing search, the poop was located in the man's climbing helmet, still clipped to the back of his harness while he enjoyed one of the most scenic restroom views of his life, near Rainier's summit crater. I was not told the rest of the story, but suffice it to say the guides didn't let the man continue without wearing his helmet, and everyone else in the group retold the story to as many appropriate audiences as they could for the rest of their lives.

We can remove many of the historical discomforts of human life through science—air conditioning, pharmaceuticals, better/lighter/ warmer/cooler outdoor gear and apparel—but when it comes down to taking a dump in the woods, we are back as our ancestors were. Except sometimes we have to put it in a blue bag and carry it around with us for a day or two.

—

3

THE INELOQUENCE
OF TALKING ABOUT THE OUTDOORS

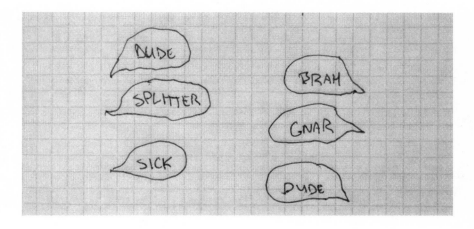

You, outdoor recreator, are quite probably quite educated: Bachelor's degree, possibly a master's degree or Ph.D. You wore a cap and gown and were handed a number of certificates decorated with fancy letters saying you went to college and finished—maybe even college for adults, which is called graduate school. But you climb rocks, or ski, or mountain bike. Shred, crush, get barreled from time to time.

In the Wednesday staff meeting, you sit up straight, sport unwrinkled business casual, and expound powerfully and authoritatively on sales figures, legal documents, strategic analyses and other data and insights. Or you teach, lawyer, guide and coach dozens of employees, design budgets of hundreds of thousands of dollars of corporate capital, and in general act like an adult.

But then on Saturday, on your bike, or at the base of a climb, or around a campfire, you're all like It Was Siiiiiiick, Brah! while pulling up on your air handlebars or making phantom hand jams in front of your face.

I know. I used to write marketing copy for an enormous software company all week, sitting in on conference calls and then architecting massive documents on how Product X will Optimize Your Company's IT Infrastructure. I would wrack my brain for multi-syllable buzzwords for hours, and then at 5 p.m. Friday, basically begin talking like "Ted" Theodore Logan, only with more F-bombs.

I'm a writer. I can afford to eat based on the idea that I can string together several hundred or thousand smart-sounding words at a time, clearly and efficiently. If I were to write the beta for a climb called Mother 1 at Vedauwoo, for inclusion in a consumer climbing magazine, it might look like this:

Mother 1 is a Vedauwoo offwidth classic, and some say it's sandbagged at 5.7+. You won't find any face holds to use outside of this flaring chicken-wing and armbar crack, so bring your offwidth technique. If you're new to offwidths, remember that an inch or two of upward progress is actually good. Be patient, place some gear, and once you get to the hand jam at the top, you're home free. Belay at the top of the crack or walk up the 5.2 R slab to the top of the Nautilus, where you can clip into two rap bolts.

But if you and I were standing at a climbing gym and I were to tell you about Mother 1, it would sound like this:

Dude, I was so fuckin scared of it I took like I think two #4s and a #5 up it. We get there and I'm totally shitting my pants at the base of the climb and I finally get on it and start wedging myself into it, and somebody said go left side in, so I did, and immediately you get in it, and it's flaring, and of course the rock has all kinds of crystals in it, but they're all facing the wrong way, down, and plus they're all fuckin greasy and polished from years of people climbing the route, and of course you have to use your whole body, so you can imagine like 50 years of skin oil all over this thing. I'm leapfrogging a 4 and a 5 all the way up, and I get higher and higher and I'm totally panicking, shaking and sweating, all like whew, whew, whew, you know that like shaky exhale when you're about to fall. And I get up to the point where the crack narrows down to a hand jam over your head, and I suck at hand jams, so I'm like fuuuuuuuck with this pathetic hand jam and trying to paw my way up the rock, just looking like a total amateur, like if I was belaying me, I'd be embarrassed for me, you know what I mean? And I somehow get in a Number One in the hand crack and I just suddenly pop out, no warning or anything, just like AAAAAAAAAA, and I think Chris had a little slack in the rope when I went, and I just cheese-grater down the rock for about 15 feet, scraping the shit out of my forearms plus I'm already bleeding from the ankles from climbing the offwidth like a goddamn grizzly bear. Anyway, I get back on it and top out, and basically go into this adrenaline-flush nap at the top as I'm sitting up there belaying. So, you know, it's not that bad.

I always wanted to be a writer, so I read great authors: Hemingway,

Fitzgerald, Gabriel Garcia Marquez, James Joyce, Steinbeck, blah blah blah. Then I went to college, then grad school. The kinds of things that increase your odds of being able to hold your own in an intellectual conversation at a dinner party.

Then I became a climber, which somehow made me less likely to quote Shakespeare, and more likely to refer to The Big Lebowski or the Beastie Boys. There are many people like me—climbers, mountain bikers, skiers, and other outdoorsfolk. Next time you're standing around a campfire, count the number of friends you have who are smart enough to (potentially) climb the corporate ladder, but dumb enough to climb mountains for "fun," able to talk in the jargon of business, but prefer to talk in the dialect of radness, at least on weekends. You probably know lots of people like that. Or maybe you are people like that?

—

4

HOW TO GET YOUR NEW BOYFRIEND/GIRLFRIEND TO HATE YOUR SPORT

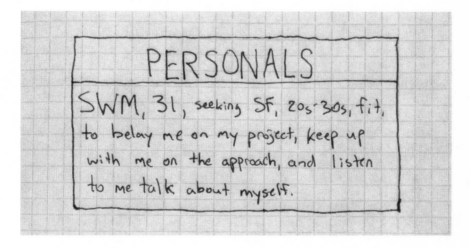

You love snowboarding. Or climbing. Or mountain biking. You've been doing it for so long, you can't remember what your life was like without it. But your new boyfriend/girlfriend doesn't—yet. So you need to teach them. Here are some tips to guarantee they'll never understand you or want to go with you, and most likely won't want to date you anymore afterward.

1. Don't start on beginner-level stuff. What, are you supposed to wait around on the bunny slopes, or some birthday-party toprope crag because your new love interest has never skied or climbed before? Pffff. Baptism by fire. Go straight to the Slickrock Trail, fuck the practice loop. You can't even remember what is was like to not be able to climb 5.10s, so start at 5.10, or 5.11.

21

2. Consider the learning environment. The best time to teach someone how to take down a sport climbing anchor is when they're at the top of the route and you're at the bottom, preferably when there are lots of other people around to listen to you yell instructions. The best place to teach mountain biking techniques is not at the trailhead, but at the steepest spot of singletrack you can find—hopefully in the middle of the day on a Saturday, when other riders can pile up behind your hesitant newbie girlfriend/boyfriend.

3. Get them to buy all the gear before they've tried the sport. Nothing puts the pressure on to learn and immediately love something like spending $2,000 on a bike, or $1,500 on skis and a season pass. This works the same way having a baby, or buying a big house, can save a failing marriage.

4. Invite all your friends to accompany the two of you on his/her first day. Think about it: When you're learning, and having a hard time, nothing beats having six or seven people waiting for you to get down a blue run as you keep falling, or having an audience to perform for when you're already nervous.

5. Remember that their first day is about them experiencing what real climbing, or skiing, or riding, is like—not learning. It's important to have them tag along on something you want to do—your project, or your ride. Instead of wasting your time teaching them footwork on a 5.5 toprope

22

route all day, drag them up a multi-pitch 5.10 with lots of hand and fist jams. Powder day? Perfect! No friends on a powder day, and that includes girlfriends and boyfriends. See you at the bottom, get some face shots, if you know what that means. Also, nothing builds character like a good crash on your first ride.

6. If you can't get them to buy all the gear beforehand, borrow ill-fitting gear for them to try. Nothing beats having a first day with ski boots that are a size too big (even better, a size too small), a climbing helmet that tilts sideways with every move, or a bike that smashes your balls every time you try to step off it.

7. Focus on the negative. Your BF doing something right? Ignore it. Point out what he's doing wrong, so he can work on it and suck less. Sigh loudly when you're doing this.

8. Tone is important. When teaching someone something new, be sure to begin all instructions with the word "just," to drive home the point that it's so simple, a 2-year-old could do it, why can't they? Examples:

"Just put the edge of your shoe on that little dime-sized nub and push off."

"Just link your turns, like I do. Are you watching me? Just do what I'm doing."

"Just grab the jug. Just grab it. Just grab the jug. Right there. Just grab it."

9. When you get tired of waiting for them, repeat "come on," as if

you were talking to a dog. You have other shit to do today besides teach

them to climb or ride. Let's go. I mean Jeeeeeeesus Christ.

—

5

HOW TO TALK SHIT
TO YOUR CLIMBING PARTNER

CHAPTER SEVEN
_____

CLIMBING COMMUNICATION
a. Belay Commands
b. Rappel Commands
c. Insults
d. Sarcastic Remarks
e. Other Jokes
f. Encouragement

"Hey, can you take photos with your phone?" I yell down from the belay to my pal Lee, as he works his way up the last 50 feet of the third pitch of Kor's Flake.

"Yeah, why?" he says, as he cleans a cam and clips it to his harness.

"I set mine down on the ground."

"When we started?"

"No, just now." I point out into the 300-some feet of air below the belay. Lee starts laughing.

Kor's Flake has a notorious offwidth on the third pitch, that you should ideally climb with two No. 6 Camalots if you want to actually protect it as

25

you climb. I had led it, walking and leapfrogging a No. 4 and a No. 5 over each other, hating life inside the slick granite gap, at different points getting my helmet, chest and crotch stuck and having to un-jam those parts by climbing down slightly. I had tossed and turned most of the previous night, wondering what it would feel like if I popped out of the offwidth at a bad spot. But I made it up without incident, and after I finished the offwidth above a tipped-out No.4 and No. 5, the moves were pure cruising, but exposed. I built a belay and blindly unclipped the carabiner holding my Metolius PAS to the back of my harness.

I heard a quick thump behind me, and thought, "Did I just drop my chalk bag?" Then I realized I had unclipped my point-and-shoot camera and let it drop, and it was probably sitting on the ground at the base of Sundance Buttress, smashed into a million pieces inside the soft case. I just shook my head and laughed. As I pulled in rope, I rehearsed what I was going to say to Lee when he got to the belay.

The conversation between Lee and I, at the expense of my camera, is how we talk when we climb: Keeping it light with sarcasm, bad jokes, gallows humor and profanity. I'm sure this is very similar to what lots of climbers experience with their partners. In fact, I hope so. If you can't crack a decent joke while you're hundreds of feet off the ground, I don't want to climb with you. Until you can.

Early in my climbing career, I was getting ready to start up a route with my friend Nick, and we had been talking about how thin the first few moves looked, and how the route might be a little bit over our heads. I chalked up, and said, "Got me on belay?"

"On belay," Nick said.

"OK, climbing."

"Not for long," Nick said.

This is what I'm talking about. Despite Nick, I got up the route without falling. I would like my partners to believe in me, but it's not entirely necessary, I guess. Sometimes I like to talk shit to them as they follow a pitch, handing out bad or fake advice, such as:

"If you can, I recommend using gription on this part."

"You can do it. If not, it's easy terrain from here, so I can just cut the rope and solo off this thing."

"Maybe you should take your shirt off for the crux."

"You can pull on that piece of gear if you can't get the moves. Remember, there's no cheating in climbing—only lying."

or, an old classic from Tom Hanson: "Try using the strength of ten men. If that doesn't work, try eleven."

I don't climb a lot of sport routes, or boulder too much, which has meant for me that people don't usually cheer you on and give encouragement as you battle your way up a route. Maybe it's because on multipitch trad routes, you can often be trying to punch through the crux when you're separated by

27

a corner, a roof, or 150 feet of rope, and you're too far away to hear any encouragement your partner might offer. When I am close enough to hear every curse word and hyperventilation as my partner battles through some tough move, I just watch and hope they don't fall. Then when they do get through it and yell something like, "I can't believe I didn't peel off right there!" I like to yell back,

"It's good that you didn't, because I just now put you on belay. Nice job."

A lot of the popular routes here in the Front Range are pretty heavily traveled, and over the years gear gets stuck in them—cams, nuts, and sometimes old pitons that are just fixed, and no one's getting out. I religiously clip fixed gear like that when I lead, partly because I want to believe that if it's been there for 10 years, it will hold me. The other part is because I like to wait until my partner gets to the next belay and ask if they cleaned that specific piece of gear, especially if it was mangled beyond belief.

"Did you get my piton out?"

or

"Whoa, where's my orange TCU? You didn't get it stuck, did you?"

I tend to gravitate towards "classics" here as well, which usually means the route was first climbed by some badass in the '50s or '60s, using far inferior gear, and far superior courage. This sometimes surfaces when I'm leading a scary-for-me pitch, and my partner will say something like

"You know, Harvey Carter led this in hobnail boots and pitons in 1954."

To which I will reply,

"Yeah, I read somewhere that he also used giant balls. Which I seem to have forgotten today."

It's important to keep things from getting too serious from the get-go—beginning with the planning of the climbing day, which begins via e-mail. If I search my e-mail correspondence with my friend Lee, I find lots of shit-talking, many times about what kind of rack we're going to bring. He usually insists on bringing three things that I don't like to climb with: Tri-Cams, hexes, and HB Offset nuts. Sometimes I say things like, "You bring the rope, I'll bring the rack. The rack is one #1 Camalot and one #2 Camalot."

And it goes on. Sometimes like this:

On Tue, May 31, 2011 at 1:05 PM, Brendan Leonard <XXXXXX@gmail.com> wrote:

How about I do the hard pitches on Kor's Flake (3, 4, and 5), and you let me lead a couple of the ones on White Whale? And then we can paper-rock-scissors for the first pitch on Enema Syringe – it's got a semi-scary, kind-of-runout slab move above a flake.

On Tue, May 31, 2011 at 2:06 PM, Lee Smith <XXXXXX@gmail.com> wrote:

How 'bout you lead everything and I sip mint juleps while I belay?

On Tue, May 31, 2011 at 2:11 PM, Brendan Leonard <XXXXXX@gmail.com> wrote:

29

I will agree to this if you bring 2 Hostess Donettes for every pitch I lead and hand them to me at the top of each one. I would prefer as close to 1/2 powdered and 1/2 chocolate as possible.

The important thing to remember is that climbing is not serious, until it gets serious. If your partner can handle it, sometimes a little shit talking can be way better than words of encouragement. Although, you can do both at the same time.

—

6

7 TIPS ON
HOW TO BE A GOOD TENTMATE

Hey, do you like camping and backpacking with your friends? Of course you do. So obviously you'd like to be invited on lots of trips. How do you get invited on lots of trips? You learn how to be a good tentmate, and make your tentmate's experience a good one. Here are a few tips on how to do that.

1. Hydrate

Drink a lot of fluids before you go to bed, to ensure you are well hydrated and able to get up to go pee plenty of times during the night. It is a good idea to put your headlamp in a location where it will be hard to locate when you need to pee, such as the bottom of your sleeping bag. When getting up to pee, maximize movement inside the tent: Don't just unzip your sleeping bag a couple inches and slide out—go all the way down to your ankles. Put on a couple jackets before you go out, maybe even some Gore-Tex. Turn your headlamp on its high setting before you do all of this. If it's snowing, leave the tent door open while you're out there doing your business.

2. Manage Your Stuff

If you have wet clothing items such as socks and shirts, put them on your tentmate's side of the tent. Pro tip: They will dry overnight if you can sneak them into his/her sleeping bag.

3. Fart

Try to eat foods that give you gas, in both quantity and volume, as well as those that produce strange and interesting smells in high intensities. Your tentmate will enjoy periodic breaks from breathing fresh mountain air, as well as trying to come up with words to describe his/her new experiences with the sense of smell. Try: Lentils, textured vegetable protein, other high-fiber foods.

4. Share The Warmth

Nothing beats spooning for maximizing bodily warmth. Especially if you're just friends. If your tentmate seems not-so-keen on the idea, explain that it's a common technique used in alpinism, and usually changes nothing in previously platonic relationships. Or say, "Dude, my nose is cold, just let me put it against your neck for a few minutes," or "Come over here, you big teddy bear."

5. Illuminate

Always keep your headlamp on its high beam, which will be helpful for reading your book long after your tentmate has shut his/her headlamp off and gone to sleep. When speaking to your tentmate, make sure to point your headlamp beam directly into his/her eyes.

6. Bring Snacks

Who wants to go all the way over to the bear canister to get a midnight snack? Grab crunchy foods to eat in your sleeping bag just in case. Corn Nuts, carrots, peanut brittle, and Doritos all make great midnight snacks.

7. Be A Good Conversationalist

In a tent, you've got a captive audience—and likely a good friend along for the trip—so take advantage. Now's the time to talk about some of your problems, fears, and worries—relationships, digestive issues, hemorrhoids. Don't you remember being a kid and staying up all night talking and goofing around at someone's slumber party? Why should the fun end just because you're an adult? I mean really, when you look back on the trip, you're not going to talk about all the fun you had sleeping. If your tentmate seems to have dozed off while you're talking to him/her, a friendly "Did you hear that? I think it was a bear" usually gets them re-engaged.

—

7

BEWARE THE URINE-DRINKING MOUNTAIN GOATS

For years, I have known to pee on rocks at high altitudes because mountain goats crave salt, and if you pee on plants, mountain goats will eat them until they're gone. I have seen goats milling around the restrooms at Summit Lake on Colorado's Mount Evans, kind of bashfully but definitely intently making their way over when they see humans stopping to pee there. The mountain goats in Washington are a little more aggressive.

I climbed the East Ridge of Ingalls Peak with my friend Jack this past August, and after topping out at 5 p.m. and descending past Ingalls Lake, we walked the trail headed back down toward Longs Pass. Just after we crossed a creek, I walked off to the side of the trail to find a rock to pee on, and started to go about my business.

It was as if the sound of my zipper was a dinner bell. A narrow white face, curious, popped over a ridge 20 feet from my crotch. Then another one. Talk about stage fright. They approached confidently. They both stared at me, and I stared back at them, confused and anxious. It was awkward, several levels above the feeling you get when you're standing at a line of urinals in the airport and you're pretty sure the guy next to you is peeking over the partition and looking at your special parts.

I don't think of myself as a prude, but you know, a little privacy is nice, even in the outdoors. Plus, a few months earlier, the National Park Service had advised hikers to not urinate near trails in Olympic National Park, after a mountain goat had attacked and killed a 63-year-old man on a trail there. It was the only known fatal mountain goat attack in the park's history. You think about these things when goats with horns are waiting for you to pee. Longingly looking at you. Like sailors who have been away at sea too long and haven't seen a woman in months.

As the two goats walked toward me, I pictured the headline, then a photo of me splayed out, pants at my ankles, having been gored to death with my pants down in the shadow of Mount Stuart as the sun set on the Enchantments. I didn't finish, or even start. I zipped my pants back up and briskly walked away. I could wait.

36

I later told my pal Fitz about the friendly mountain goats, and he said, Yeah, I was on a trip once and one of the guys on the trip told this story about peeing directly into a goat's mouth, like he was a human water fountain.

I laughed, said That's amazing. And then I felt a little dirty.

A few weeks later, I sat on my friend Steve's couch in Seattle as he flipped through photos from years of alpine climbing in the Cascades on his laptop. It was an amazing collection of adventures and stories, and I'm sure I could have sat there for three hours and listened to him.

Then, there they were, the goats, in a photo on Steve's laptop. The same look of longing, the curious piss-thirst, in a similar alpine environment.

"These goats would come right up to you when you were peeing," Steve said.

"I know, man, they did that the time I climbed Ingalls Peak with my buddy Jack," I said. "It freaked me out. I walked away."

"Oh, they'll come right up and drink pee directly from your stream," he said. "I peed right into a mother goat's mouth, just standing there lapping it up."

Jesus Christ.

"It was the closest thing to porn I've ever done. I think I have a photo of it here somewhere."

8

ARE YOU READY FOR YOUR SUMMIT PHOTO?

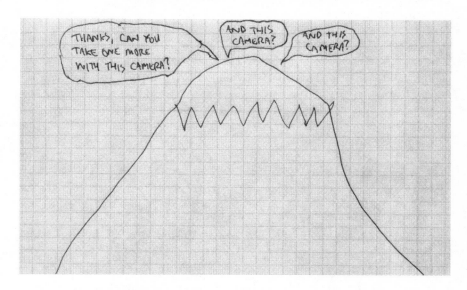

Are you going hiking this weekend? Planning a climb of Mount Hood, Shasta, Rainier? There are two things you should be doing: training, and planning what your summit photo is going to look like. Here are a few things to think about:

1. What are you going to do with your hands?

a. thumbs up

b. gang signs

c. throw the horns

d. throw the horns and add the extra thumb (which means "I love you" instead of "so metal")

    e. Something awkward

    f. shaka

    g. double shaka

    h. hold a pair of coconuts

2. Decide on the mood. Is everyone going to smile? No? Well, are you all going to look tough, like you did in your high school football team photo? Important.

3. Is your helmet crooked?

4. Try to display as much gear as possible so people viewing the photo will know you got into some serious shit up there. Ice axe, trekking poles, headlamp even if you didn't use it—basically empty out your pack and hang everything off your person. Yeah. Now you look like what's-his-name who climbed the Eiger really fast, Ueli Steck or whatever.

5. Are you jumping? That's cool too, as long as your friend operating the camera can catch you at the top of your trajectory. If not, repeat it as many times as necessary to get the shot. I am not joking, I don't care if you have to jump in the air 40-something times in the thin air above 12,000 feet. Start yelling "GODAMMIT, JIM" or whatever your friend's name is after jump #20, and then maybe they'll start to get it.

6. It's not a bad idea to have someone take a shot of you by yourself, preferably looking pensive. Do you know how to look pensive?

Just gaze away from the camera into the distance and think about some heavy shit, like how many rocks you're standing on (I mean, for real) or whose new baby is going to be your favorite, Kim Kardashian's or Kate Middleton's.

7. Other props: If you bring a beer to the summit, everyone who sees your summit photo will know it was a pretty casual climb for you. If you bring a watermelon, everyone will know you are a badass, and hilarious. Make sure you bring something to cut the watermelon with.

8. Do you do yoga? Now's the time. Only question is which pose. Savasana, Plow Pose and Happy Baby are always aesthetic and complementary of beautiful backdrops.

—

9

HEY COFFEE, I LOVE YOU

When you go on a climbing or backpacking trip and someone says, **"I'll bring the coffee,"** do you secretly bring your own stash to supplement whatever they're bringing, because you know you're going to drink double the amount of coffee they think you're going to drink, and then some? I do too. This is not a control issue; it is a coffee issue.

Do you like coffee? Do you LOVE coffee? How much? Of course, it is not quantifiable. It's like saying you're the "#1 Fan" of an NFL football team, which is, of course, not validated by any ranking system. If coffee were a football team, I would be that shirtless guy standing in the end zone stands with my entire body and head painted to match my team's uniform, going completely batshit for all three televised hours, as if my actions could help my team win. Coffee fuels nearly everything I do in the outdoors, and 100% of the writing I do.

Sometimes I get headaches from not drinking enough coffee. When I am high up on a climbing route and I am calculating how much more time we have until the sun goes down, I perhaps should be worried about things like rappelling down in the dark. Instead I am anxious about more coffee. Will there be a coffee shop open on the way home? If not, where's the closest convenience store? Will they have coffee, or do they stop making it in the late afternoon? I have several times before spent all day climbing in Eldorado Canyon, sweating my ass off in the sun, and immediately afterward rushed to the Eldorado Market to sit outside and two-fist Gatorade and coffee until I become less of a grizzly bear.

Halfway is all the further I can make it anywhere in the outdoors before I start thinking about my next cup of coffee. We're at the top of the climb, all the scary leads are done and all we have to do is walk off or rappel down. We're at the summit of a peak, and ready to turn around and start making our way back to the car. I am thinking about coffee. Where is the good shit, the check-up from the neck up. I am serious. Look at my face. Espresso, french press, drip, pourover. I must have it. I must have it now.

Some people hate Starbucks. I battle with this. Part of me thinks lots of Big Corporate things are bad, but a bigger part of me enjoys the fact that I can get a cup of strong coffee in many places in America that I couldn't 20 years ago. Of course, on the road, I don't mind truck stop coffee. It is not the best, but given no other options, I will drink the shit out of that shit. It reminds me a little bit of real coffee.

I have battled a couple addictions in life, and won handily. I am proud of this. I am addicted to coffee, and I am not going to battle it. I am going to embrace it. Last spring, I had stomach pains that my doctor said were either an ulcer or gastritis. He asked how much coffee I drank every day, and I told him, 32 to 40 ounces. He said I might think about decreasing my coffee consumption. I nodded and said OK while a little man inside me made a mean face at him and gave him the finger.

One time last summer when my friend Tommy and I got up hella early to do a climb in Tuolumne, we skipped breakfast, but I mixed together cold water, protein powder and Starbucks Via in a 14-ounce Nalgene bottle and chugged it on the drive to the trailhead. Tommy said he would rather skip coffee than drink cold coffee. I was like, What are you, some kind of savage.

My grandmother is 84 years old, and when we are together for the holidays, I will routinely make a pot of coffee at 7 p.m. after dinner. I ask my grandmother, Grandma, if I make some coffee, will you drink some? She has never said no. My grandmother is awesome.

I paid $9 for a single cup of Japanese siphon coffee a couple weeks ago. It was worth it. Believe it or not, some of the best coffee I've had in the western U.S. is at the Bellagio Buffet in Las Vegas. As my pal Jayson said to me, "Leonard, I'd pay 40 bucks just to drink coffee and eat dessert at the Bellagio." I would too.

You know what the halfway point is on a Rim-to-Rim hike or run in the Grand Canyon? Some people would say the Colorado River, since it's the bottom of the canyon. In my mind, it is Phantom Ranch, where a cup of not-that-bad coffee is $2. Of which I will pound two before continuing up to the South Rim. If each cup were $15, I would pay that at the bottom of the Grand Canyon, where coffee is an unexpected luxury and a privilege.

—

10

HOW TO BARK DOWN A DOG

Maybe you only ask yourself this question while bicycling or running: Can I beat up that dog?

When it comes down to it and a dog is chasing you, you start to calculate your odds of survival if the dog actually attacks you. Most breeds, you think yeah, maybe I could. Not pit bulls or dobermans, but many dogs, I'd give myself at least 1:2 odds.

Career runners and cyclists have usually had at least one run-in with an aggressive dog, whether it's a full-on attack or just being barked at and chased. When you're getting chased, you never know if that dog is going to catch you, and what he or she is going to do if he or she catches you.

47

I was chased by several dozen dogs on my bike tour across the mostly rural southern United States last year, and I can tell you, everyone has their methods to deal this phenomenon. One couple we met used pepper spray on every single dog that aggressively approached them. Two recumbent cross-country tourers carried cut-off broomsticks that they would swing, and sometimes hit dogs with. We had a friendlier method, squirting the dogs with water bottles, and my aim was starting to get pretty dead-on, when one day, I discovered a far better method that didn't waste any water: Barking.

Nothing proved to be more effective, cathartic and satisfying on our trip than barking at the collective aggressive dogs of Texas, Louisiana, Mississippi, Alabama and northern Florida. It also marked, for me, the point on the trip when we just said Fuck it, this is not normal behavior, but this is what we're doing now, after a couple thousand miles of pedaling all day. And I guess I liked that.

I'd like to share what I learned. This is how you bark down a dog that's chasing you.

I mean really, all you're doing here is beating the dog at his or her own game. You have to take their tool/weapon, turn that shit up to 11, and deliver it all at once. The dog has probably heard all kinds of things from its owner, trying to get it to calm down: A stern command, maybe a yank of the leash, choke collar, etc. Easy, buddy. Stop barking at the cyclists/runners/UPS employee, Buster. Heel. Bad dog.

What the dog has not seen is a human being going FUCKING CRAZY on it. Which is what you're going to do. For one second. When the dog realizes you have completely lost your shit, he or she will be shocked. You are unstable, possibly dangerous. Ideally, the dog will stop chasing you.

First thing: How loud are you capable of yelling? Think about this. On a windy day, 200 feet from your climbing partner, how loud would you yell "on belay?" OK, add 20 percent to that. Pretend your significant other is about to be hit by a bullet train, and they're 200 feet away from you. How loud would you yell now? See, that's how loud you're going to bark at this dog, which is going to be 10-15 feet away from you when you do it.

The volume curve on this has to start at 100%. It's a bark. You have to startle the dog, not give it a chance to understand what's coming. Don't think of what a motorcycle sounds like as it passes you on the highway, with the Doppler effect. Think of a bomb going off next to your bed, where your alarm clock usually sits.

This is "HEY!" Not "heeeeyyyYYYYY!!!"

All right then. Call up all your frustration, anger and sadness from the last month of your life. You didn't get a raise, your boyfriend said those pants make you look fat, your girlfriend asked you if your hairline was receding, someone cut you off in traffic, all that stuff. Anger is repressed sadness, so take that sadness, and turn it into anger now. You will have one second to get all that rage out.

Take in one, quick, sharp breath, and

DELIVER.

Say whatever word you want, drop the F-bomb, your ex-wife's name, whatever. Keep it to one syllable, though. I prefer a simple "HEY"—but in capital letters so big they are unable to be displayed on the printed page. Remember, you are screaming in those gigantic capital letters, not starting low and building. Be a that bomb going off, no warning. Be confident in your bark, and visualize knocking the dog on his/her ass with the sudden volume of it.

Then, watch what happens. The dog should look confused, as if he or she just watched you turn into a grizzly bear on a bicycle. And if you're riding next to someone, they might say something like my pal Tony said to me one morning riding on a country road in Florida:

"OK dude, I gotta admit, I shit my pants a little bit on that one."

All but twice, this worked for me. Both times, a rotweiler was chasing us as we tried to pedal uphill. I was genuinely scared. This is maybe the time you get out the pepper spray. Or, you know, a cattle prod.

Practice a little bit, but certainly nowhere public. I hope it works as well for you as it did for me.

—

11

ADVANCED TECHNIQUES FOR THE WELL-ROUNDED ROCK CLIMBER

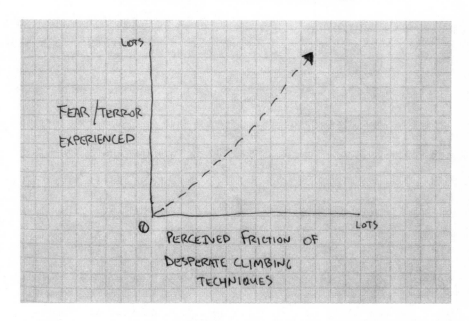

I don't know if Tom Hanson, the Commissioner of Castlewood Canyon, made it up, but he said to me once, "There's no cheating in climbing—only lying." I'm sure you're familiar with graceful and sexy techniques like gastoning, flagging, and heel hooking. Here are some even sexier techniques to add to your repertoire:

Assisted Foot Lift: What's the matter, you can't pull off the full lotus in your yoga class? Neither can I. I can barely sit cross-legged on the ground without getting hip cramps. Well, when you're climbing and you see an awesome foothold right next to your hip, but you don't want to pull the 2 or

3 moves it will take to put yourself in position to use it, just use the Assisted Foot Lift. Lift your leg as high as you can, oh, you're probably still 6 inches short of the foothold, but no worries. Reach down with one hand, grab your shoe (shoelaces if it's really desperate), and give your foot a little boost to get it up on the foothold.

Tree Jug/Tree Smear: There are two popular climbing techniques that involve trees. As you might guess, most decent trees are found on trad routes. There is almost no better handhold that wrapping one hand (or both hands) around a tree trunk and yarding on it to gain some upward progress. This is the Tree Jug. Obviously, your choice to use one or both hands depends on the circumference of the tree. Sometimes you just have to say to yourself, "Climbing this rock shit is hard. The hell with it, I'm using this tree." The Tree Smear is a move wherein you stand on a branch, or trunk, of a tree, to gain upward progress.

Full Body Scum: This involves smashing your entire body against the rock and pulling upward with your hands, using the friction your body and clothes create to substitute for trying to stand on some tiny footholds. Particularly useful if there are chickenheads that you can hook the waistbelt of your harness on and take a second to contemplate your next move.

Belly Flop: Hate scary mantel moves? Then don't try to lift your feet up once you've committed. If you have enough space on the ledge you're *supposed* to mantel onto, just lean your upper body forward until you tip onto the ledge. Then you can shimmy your legs up, or bring one leg up onto the ledge and kind of roll over. I believe I saw Chris Sharma do this once in a video of him on one of his 5.15a routes, but don't quote me.

No-Hands-No-Feet Rest: You've heard of the "no-hands" rest, in which one comes to a point on a climb where the angle of the rock and the footholds combine for an opportunity for the climber to shake out both hands at the same time before continuing up. Sometimes it involves a knee bar, which is rad when you're hanging upside down. Well, the No-Hands-No-Feet rest is like that, but not nearly as cool. Say you are on a trad climb and you're pulling some moves, maybe up a chimney-like feature, and a big ledge appears to your left or your right. To execute the No-Hands-No-Feet Rest, simply flop your ass up onto the ledge like you're hopping up to sit on your kitchen counter at home. Then chill. If it's a big enough ledge, you can lie down, maybe eat that Snickers bar in your pocket, smoke a cig, whatever.

Head Jam: I've never tried this one. It's usually used to overcome wacky roofs on old-school trad routes, like Cozyhang in Boulder Canyon. It's not so much a jam, as much as using the strength of your neck to get a little extra oomph to get up and over the hump.

The Telegraph: You may have done this while leading a climb before. You are pumped. You have two OK handholds and one foothold about the size of a dime. You are barely hanging onto the wall. You need to move your other foot up onto a decent foothold, but you feel like the slightest movement (or even a 2 mph breeze) will throw off your precarious balance and pop you off the wall. It's OK. Know what I like to do? Hyperventilate, and do The Telegraph. Take that foot you absolutely desperately need to move onto the foothold, and tap the toe of your climbing shoe up the wall towards the foothold—every 2 inches, every 4 inches, whatever—mapping out an invisible dotted line until you reach the foothold. Voila! Doesn't that feel better?

The Cam Stand: Are you like 99% of sane climbers, who hate climbing offwidths, but sometimes you find yourself leading one? Well, when it gets desperate and you're all smashed into that crack, plug in a No. 4 or No. 5 Camalot as low as you can, and stand on that thing. Oh yeah. No-Hands Rest. The Cam Stand is probably not good for your cams, but it might keep you from vomiting on yourself in the offwidth.

Crying: Don't be ashamed. If you're leading, and it's so desperate that the only thing you can think about is hugging your mom, go ahead and let the waterworks flow. Usually your partner can't see your face or the tears from below, and if you're far enough above him or her, they might not even see your body convulsing with sobs. If they do, and mention it when you're both at the next belay, tell them no, you were dry heaving because you think you ate something bad last night. Or say something like, "No way, dude, I was laughing. That's how desperate it was. I just lost it."

12

ANNOUNCING A NEW LINE OF INVISIBLE CLIMBING OUTERWEAR

Fact: Shirts are for suckers. They're heavy, hot, and if you wear one when you're rock climbing, the ladies (or dudes, as it were) can't see your back muscles when you're sending your project.

Well hey, not announced at the Outdoor Retailer Winter Market is a revolutionary new piece of climbing outerwear:

It's INVISICOOL, a revolutionary new invisible new game-changing fabric that's new and revolutionary: It's invisible. It's nearly weightless, at less than one ounce (Men's Large). It uses your body's sweat to cool, your body. As you sweat, sweat coats your skin. When sweat evaporates, it cools. That's where INVISICOOL fabric comes in: It doesn't do anything to your sweat, enabling it to cool, your body.

The proper spelling of INVISICOOL is "INVISICOOL," in all capital letters. INVISICOOL blocks 0% of incoming UVA and UVB rays.

INVISICOOL shirts are now available in short-sleeve ($29.95), long-sleeve ($34.95), tank top (women's only, $29.95) and turtleneck ($39.95). A dickie will be introduced this fall.

INVISICOOL shirts were designed for hard sport climbing and bouldering, when extra ounces—and appearing shirtless—really matter. But that's not all. INVISICOOL aren't just for the crag or the gym. You can wear them anywhere being half-naked is appropriate, for any activity:

- Cycling

- Going to the beach

- Going to the nude beach

- Shirts vs. Skins recreational basketball games

- Mowing your lawn

- Yelling at arresting officers when you're drunk in your front yard

- AND MORE!

BUT WAIT THERE'S MORE CHECK OUT THESE

TESTIMONIALS FROM JUST A FEW OF OUR ~~DOZENS~~ MILLIONS

OF SATISFIED CUSTOMERS

"I never crush boulders in anything but my INVISCOOL shirts."

-Steve Denny, Ragged Mountain Sports, Carbondale, Colo.

"Can you execute a completely superfluous heel hook on toprope while wearing something other than an INVISICOOL tank top? Maybe, but why would you?"

-Amanda Villeme

"Actually, I call it my 'Man Catcher Tank Top,' thanks very much."

-Hillary Nitschke

"I've actually been working on a prototype of invisible climbing shirts since the late 1970s. Congratulations, INVISICOOL, for making it happen!"

-Malcolm Daly, founder of Trango, founding member of The Access Fund

WHAT ARE YOU WAITING FOR, CALL NOW

—

13

LOSE WEIGHT NOW WITH THE 10,000-FOOT DIET

Hey

Are you sick and tired of diets that JUST DON'T WORK?

Do you feel like a sucker after losing a few pounds with the NEWEST WEIGHT LOSS PRODUCT, but not seeing results after the first few days?

Well, maybe it's time to try a real solution that's guaranteed: THE 10,000-FOOT DIET.

Brought to you by the same people who invented POOPING IN A HOLE IN THE GROUND and SLEEPING ON A ONE-INCH THICK MATTRESS, the 10,000-FOOT DIET has been proven to work by expedition climbers, long-distance backpackers and thru-hikers, and will work for you.

Listen up, Man-Boobs: Do you have a week of vacation you'd like to dedicate to losing those pesky last few pounds, getting rid of those love handles and that ass-fat, and turning yourself into a shredded, cut, human beast? Forget those surgeries, those meal-replacement bars and shakes, forget meth—the 10,000-FOOT DIET works, with no adverse side effects.

We'll help you achieve your DREAM BODY with 4 SIMPLE STEPS:

1. Walk into the wilderness.

2. Carry all your food in a backpack.

2. Walk 10 miles a day at high altitudes.

3. Cook all your meals in a single pot on a one-burner stove.

AND WATCH

THE POUNDS

MELT AWAY

You'll enjoy a breakfast of oatmeal and instant coffee before your lung-busting days of walking with a 40-pound backpack on your back. What's for breakfast the next morning? Certainly not fresh croissants, or toasted bagels with cream cheese, with a steaming-hot vanilla latte. No, you'll enjoy another breakfast of oatmeal and instant coffee.

While walking miles and miles of steep terrain all day, you'll snack on Bars That Kind Of Remind You Of Food And Are Pretty Tasty Until You've Eaten Two Every Day For Six Days And Now You're Fuckin Sick Of Them. Mmmm. Atop a mountain somewhere, you may say to your hiking partner, "Wow, these really taste like the chocolate chip cookies my grandmother used to make," and when he or she says, "Really?" You'll reply "Hell no!" and cackle hysterically.

At dinner, you'll ravenously tear into pasta dishes that taste amazing when you're 15 miles from the nearest road, but even you might have turned your nose up at when you were a drunk college sophomore.

We'll help you lose all that desk-jockey weight in a few short days, or a couple weeks, with something we call MATH:

calories consumed – calories burned = your unwanted pounds

disappearing

Who can gain weight when they're burning 6,000 calories a day and only eating 3,000? Certainly not you. Grab your pack, cinch that waistbelt around your spare tire, and take our CUSTOM KIND-OF TASTY MEAL PLANS INTO THE BACKCOUNTRY NOW.

CALL TODAY

—

14

THE GREATEST MOUNTAINEERING SURVIVAL STORY NEVER TOLD

A few years ago, I climbed Drift Peak near Leadville, Colorado, on Presidents Day with my friend Aaron and my friend Lee. Lee had started up the peak a couple times before in the winter, but bailed for different reasons. He had promised if we made it to the summit with him on what would be his first successful winter ascent of the peak, he'd tell me the story of how the mountain had "almost killed" him. I expected, of course, another story like the time he was climbing the northwest face of Torreys Peak by himself in the winter and a rock came screaming down the mountain, slamming into his foot and breaking three bones. He had to glissade down 800 feet, then use his ski poles as crutches to hike out 2.5

miles to his truck, and drive home to Littleton, where he almost drove through the back wall of his garage because he couldn't get his smashed foot to push the clutch in time.

The Drift Peak story wasn't quite like that. As we descended the snowy ridge, I was quietly satisfied I had made the summit without throwing up. Lee had the energy of the Kool-Aid Man. He darted past Aaron and me, yelling, ""Gather 'round, Girl Scouts, it's time for a story!"
There he was, he said, not too far from where we were sitting, by himself on a cold December day in 2000. He was planning on climbing Fletcher Mountain, a half-mile further up past the summit of Drift Peak. He trudged up the snowy ridge, and at the point where the final summit slopes begin, he came up on a notch in the ridge. He'd have to climb down a 40-foot slope, then up a 60-foot slope, to regain the ridge. The second slope was high-angle and looked ripe for an avalanche.

Lee turned around to go home and live to climb another day. The ridge, after all, is colloquially known as "Villa Ridge," named after a man killed by an avalanche on it. Lee made his way back down the ridge and stopped on top of a large snow dome to eat lunch. It was 11 o'clock in the morning.

He jammed the spike of his ice axe into the hard snow and tied his pack to it, anchoring it so it wouldn't slide away. He opened his pack and pulled from it his absolute favorite mountain lunch: A ham-and-cheese sandwich on whole wheat, with mayonnaise and mustard.

This, Girl Scouts, is the "No shit, there I was" part of the story.

Munching on his sandwich, enjoying the view to the south of the Sawatch Range, Lee stopped breathing. He tried to cough, but nothing. His airway was completely blocked by a piece of sandwich. He hacked. Nothing. After 10 or so seconds of desperately trying to draw in some thin, 12,900-foot-high air, he began to see a gray frame at the very edge of his vision. He realized he had wasted a lot of time.

He had survived 35 years of pushing his limits in the big hills, including hundreds of pitches of roped climbing, that rock on Torreys Peak, the occasional incompetent partner, stuck ropes, Rocky Mountain thunderstorms, and he was about to be killed by a goddamn ham sandwich. His story in the next year's Accidents In North American Mountaineering would be hard to frame as "heroic."

In 1974, American physician Henry J. Heimlich popularized a series of abdominal thrusts that came to be known as "The Heimlich Maneuver," a technique that has saved the lives of many humans who neglect to chew their food completely. The light bulb went on in Lee's oxygen-deprived brain and he remembered the self-Heimlich technique, in which a choking person can Heimlich themselves by leaning over, say, the back of a restaurant chair and pushing it into their diaphragm.

There are no chairs on the northwest ridge of Drift Peak.

But what about leaning the spike of his ice axe on a rock and driving the head of it into his abdomen? Lee looked around. Nothing but snow, which would just give way under his weight. He would have to glissade down the ridge to a talus field 40 feet away to find a large rock. If he could make it in time.

The gray circle around his vision grew larger, and the tunnel of beautiful Colorado mountain scenery shrank. Sixty percent vision now. He frantically fiddled with the knot attaching his ice axe to his pack. Come on come on come on. It came free. His pack shot down the slope in front of him. Still, no air.

Lee ripped the ice axe out of the snow and pushed himself into a butt-slide down the slope. He planted the head of his ice axe underneath his ribcage, adze pointing right, pick pointing left. His chest sucked itself into a knot, starving for oxygen.

He picked up speed, lifting his feet in the air so his crampon points didn't catch. His vision tunneled down to 25 percent. At the end of that tunnel was a rock shaped like the state of Tennessee, pointing straight up in the air, flat side facing Lee.

His last thought was, "I'm aiming for Memphis." Just before slamming into the rock, his vision went black. He passed out. Well, he assumes he passed out, because he doesn't remember hitting anything.

He woke up on his back, sucking in air in big gulps, holding a round ball of ham, cheese, mayo, mustard and whole wheat bread in his mouth. He spit it out.

Everything hurt: stomach, chest, back, shoulders – his hair hurt. Lying on his back, the Tennessee-shaped rock sat a foot and a half behind his head. The Rocky Mountain Self-Heimlich had worked. Near as he could tell, the piece of sandwich had dislodged when his ice axe hit the rock, and the head of the ice axe compressed his diaphragm.

Or, it popped out of his throat when he flopped onto his back after doing a full somersault over the rock. While completely unconscious.

Either way, two thoughts popped into his head: "I could have died." And, "But I didn't."

Sitting there on the ridge eight years later with Aaron and me, Lee closed his story, saying, "And I never told anybody that story, because if my wife found out, she never would have let me go climbing again."

To which I replied, "Or eat ham sandwiches by yourself." If not for the unfortunate but amicable dissolution of Lee's marriage, he may have taken that story to the grave—in his journal for the day, he recorded it simply as "an interesting day."

—

15

ARE YOU A BEAUTIFUL
AND UNIQUE SNOWFLAKE?

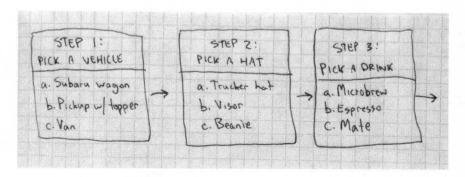

I told my friend Dan I was getting tired of having long hair, that I often fantasized about trimming all of it off and leaving just a quarter-inch, fantasized about 90-second showers, no messing with ponytails under helmets, knots, conditioner, paying for haircuts.

Dan, a curly-haired man himself who has more than once used the word "inspire" when describing Rob Machado's bro-fro, said, "You should dread it."

I said Nah, I'm already a long-haired, sandal-wearing vegetarian rock climber. With Colorado license plates. On my van. That I live in. Shouldn't we all have a limit on our number of cultural stereotype check boxes?

You ever feel like you might not be so unique, that maybe you're just wearing the uniform of a specific subculture? Ever walked up to a station wagon with a rack on top of it in the parking lot of a ski hill or trailhead, and then realized it was someone else's station wagon with a rack on top? Whoops.

Sometime I catch myself (1) buying granola and organic yogurt in (2) Whole Foods, sporting a (3) ponytail and (4) Chacos and carrying my groceries out in a backpack instead of a plastic bag (5), and in that backpack is a (6) reusable water bottle and (7) coffee mug, and I get in my van with a (8) rocket box and (9) mountain bike on top of it, and the shuffle on my ipod picks a song from a (10) Bob Marley box set to play—well, I gotta scratch my chin and wonder: Am I myself, or am I exactly like Every Other Dude Who Wants To Be A Mountain Dude?

I used to help lead backpacking trips for inner-city kids, and on one of the trips, we all hopped out of the van at the trailhead in the Wallowa Mountains, and we discussed the food. One of the other adult volunteers said something about a vegetarian in the group, and one of the teenagers, Miguel, said Who's a vegetarian, and I said I am. He looked at my sandals and said,

Do you drive a Subaru?

I laughed and said yes, I do. Pegged.

I volunteered with another group in California, and the other trip leader, Darin, and I, both flew out from Denver to pick up the kids in the Bay Area and head out for a week in the backcountry. Darin and I had met for the first time only days before and got along well. On the third day of the trip, Darin and I realized we were wearing almost the exact same outfit, down to the same brand of headlamp. The two white guys from Colorado, unintentionally perpetuating Colorado (ahem, Colo-rad-bro) stereotypes.

My friend Jarrett asked me one time what I thought about a guy who was walking past us sporting a foot-high mohawk and full punk regalia, and I said I think it's great that he's doing his own thing. Jarrett said, Is he really doing his own thing, or is he wearing a uniform of people who love punk? I think about that sometimes. Then I think about how much I love wearing my smelly, beat-up black soft shell everywhere including restaurants with cloth napkins, and how much more I love to talk to people about rock climbing and national park trails than who's dating who or reality TV or whatever.

Fellow dirt-lover: Put on your (1) puffy jacket with the duct-tape patches and get in your (2) all-wheel-drive station wagon/pickup with a topper, and we can fist bump at the (3) non-corporate coffee shop/Banff Mountain Film Festival World Tour stop/crag/trailhead sometime, and (4) use the word "gnar" as a noun. I will be pleased to meet your (5) dog named Kaya and perhaps later buy you a (6) microbrew so we can exchange more (7) beta. Please be advised that I (8) do not shower that often.

—

16

DO YOU HAVE OBSESSIVE CAMPFIRE ADJUSTMENT SYNDROME?

Do you ever stare at a burning pile of logs and find yourself unable to stop futzing with it? Do you look at a campfire and immediately see one or more ways you could improve it? Are you the guy or girl sitting closest to the fire, always wearing a pair of beat-up leather gloves, or holding a narrow piece of split log, so you can adjust the infrastructure according to your next whim?

If you answered "yes" to any of these three questions, you may have Obsessive Campfire Adjustment Syndrome, or O.C.A.S. Obsessive Campfire Adjustment Syndrome affects one out of every four camping enthusiasts in their lifetime, which means you have a 25 percent chance of developing symptoms. It also means the next time you go camping in a group of four, three of you will enjoy the campfire, contentedly staring into its embers like cave people, and one of you will not stop messing with the goddamn fire.

Ask yourself:

Are you able to just sit and enjoy a campfire for what it is, a source of light and heat in the dark, cold night? If you answered No, you may have O.C.A.S.

Do you think you, not the wind, can control the direction that campfire smoke blows? If you answered Yes, you may have O.C.A.S.

Have you ever put a huge log on the fire, then gone to bed five minutes later, leaving someone else with the responsibility of making sure the fire goes out? This is not a symptom, but it is kind of a dick move, and you should probably stop doing it.

Sufferers of OCAS may not show symptoms until their mid-30s or early 40s. People with OCAS may not know they have OCAS. Symptoms may only surface when someone with OCAS is on a date.

If you suspect a friend may have OCAS, it is your responsibility to confront them. Try saying things like, "Dave, why don't you sit down and stop fucking with the damn fire?"

Talk to your doctor about OCAS today. You're not alone. Many sufferers of OCAS have gone on to enjoy a lifetime of weekend campfires without so much as even adding wood when the fire is about to go out.

Ask your doctor about which OCAS treatment options are right for you. Stop worrying, and start enjoying campfires today. If you have trouble concentrating, or have an erection lasting four hours or more, that probably has nothing to do with OCAS.

—

THE MASOCHIST'S GUIDE TO BUSHWHACKING

#12. Bushwhacking builds ——————.
a. character
b. resilience
c. anger

"Bushwhacking is like my third favorite thing to do in the outdoors, behind crotch-deep postholing and getting hit in the head by falling rocks," I said, shoulder-deep in desert foliage, hands raised like a man fending off a swarm of bees, walking forward in sloppy, almost-balanced steps.

I am not a fan of bushwhacking, but somehow practice it more often than things I like to do. Often by accident. It often begins with the utterance of the phrase, "The directions say 'Find the faint climbers' trail …'" Perhaps you have had a similar experience while hiking, backpacking, mountaineering, canyoneering: ducking, pushing branches aside with your hands, dead limbs tearing at your clothes and catching your backpack straps, thorns scratching exposed skin, pushing through thick vegetation in hopes of finding open terrain in a few feet. You know, fun.

Bushwhacking, although probably no one's preferred method of backcountry travel, is a necessary skill, and not even so much a skill as a way of thinking. You are not doing it so much as you are withstanding it. Attitude is important. It is OK to hate it, and it is OK to love it—although if you say you love it, 100% of people will ask you what the hell is wrong with you, which is correct.

There are a couple things I like to remember about bushwhacking, which make it at least tolerable to do, and sometimes funny to reflect on weeks afterward, long after the scratches on your legs and arms have healed:

Bushwhacking is still exercise, and therefore at the end of the day, you can still drink as much beer and eat as much food as you want. Maybe you never made it to the climb you wanted to do, or alpine lake you wanted to sit next to and enjoy a pimiento sandwich with your toes in the cool water— who cares? You battled vegetation, pushing forward in a sometimes foolishly uphill direction, for minutes, even hours. You will have the bacon cheeseburger, fries, and two IPAs, both brought to the table now, thank you. I have spent entire days bushwhacking, completely unable to find a ridge on a peak or a rock formation in the forest. It was dumb, but it was still physical activity.

You are never "lost." Just as your father, never lost on a family road trip, refusing to stop and ask for directions, you will find your way. Pick a direction and follow it. It will lead to something—a stream, a trail, a lake, a high point from which you can see the surrounding terrain, or sometimes, another hour of bushwhacking, which can be very Zen if you approach it with the right attitude. You will eventually find some feature you can identify on a map. Oh, do you not have a map? Sorry, you actually might be lost.

There is no style to bushwhacking. It's like postholing, or shoveling dirt. No one will make a four-minute film about your bushwhack for the Banff Mountain Film Festival. No one will stand behind you and give you beta and cheer you on, "Yeah Bob, grab that branch, drop your right knee, step up …" Just get in that shit and start pushing.

When you put your helmet on, real bushwhacking begins. Pretty simple rule here. If you are bushwhacking through thick foliage and you have a climbing helmet in or on your backpack instead of on your head, you are half-assing it. With a helmet on, you gain a third more brute force. It's like those old snowplows they used to put on train engines. A hard shell on your head beats that soft flesh on your arms any day. Put your head down and go for it.

Vegetation is not quite your friend, not quite your enemy. You will sometimes grab branches to pull yourself uphill, hold them to lower yourself down gullies, and hang on for balance. Sometimes they will hit you in the face. You will pull thorns out of your hands and thighs. You will accidentally break branches, and other branches will repeatedly untie your shoelaces. Do not show remorse or fear. Plants can smell weakness, and they will team up on you like an NFL defensive line until they bring you down. You are better than them. That is why we have a dish called "salad."

—

18

BIG SHOUT-OUT TO ROCKS

It is a fact that if you are reading this, there is a 75 percent chance you have touched at least one rock in the past 21 days. With your hands, feet, bicycle tires, you have interacted with rocks in some manner.

One hundred percent of mountains are made out of rocks, and most trails feature rocks quite prominently. If something in the outdoors is not a plant, animal, water, or rock, it is dirt, which is basically a bunch of tiny rocks.

Rocks are good for all kinds of fun things:

- You can walk on them

- You can ride your bike on them

- If you are a rock climber, you can crimp, smear, edge on their features, or jam your hands, feet, fists, fingers and arm-bars in their

cracks

- You can marvel at their hugeness

- You can navigate a raft or kayak between them

- You can build a fort out of them

- You can take photos of them

- You can skip them across docile bodies of water

- You can make sculptures of naked ancient Romans out of them

- or naked Greeks

Rocks and I had a big year last year. Not quite as big a year as my laptop

and I did, but pretty big. I climbed several mountains, which I noted at the

top were in fact really just big piles of rocks. I traveled halfway around the

world to climb foreign rocks a couple times, and noted similarities to

domestic rocks. I slept at least one night with some rocks jabbing me in the

back, and only got hit by a couple small ones falling on my helmeted head at

bullet-like speeds. I'm pretty sure I broke a bone in my wrist accidentally

flying over my handlebars onto a rock in Sedona in March, and I get a little

pissed about that, until I remember how many times I sat on rocks to eat

lunch and energy bars. Then I'm like, Man, rocks are like my favorite thing to

sit on when I'm outside. Obviously chairs are better, but I am not hauling a

goddamn chair up to the top of a mountain every time I want to sit down, that's for sure.

Sometimes people like to talk about things that changed the game in rock climbing. They mention cams, sticky rubber, chalk, and their favorite climbers, like the guy who invented pitons or the guy who brought sport climbing to America or the other guy who invented yelling "TSAAAAAT" when you're trying hard. Hey, you know what makes climbing really rad?

Rocks. I mean, when people are onstage accepting their Golden Piton Awards every fall, they really should thank the fans, their heroes, and the rock, for making it all possible. Big up to my man El Cap.

If you like rocks, the outdoors is totally the place to be. Mountains, for instance, contain a large amount of rocks, as you may have noticed if you've been up high in places like Colorado, Utah, California, or Montana. Seriously, try to count them next time you're on a summit—you'll be like One, two, three ... aw, hell, "a lot."

If you had fun in the outdoors this year, take a minute to thank a rock.

And if you haven't had a chance to interact with rocks recently, check them out this weekend. Yes, carpet and hardwood floors are nice, but no one ever built a national park around them.

———

19

DON'T SANDBAG ME, BRO

★ OFFICIAL ★

SANDBAGGING CONVERSION CHART

GRADE YOU TELL A SANDBAGGER YOU CLIMB	GRADE SANDBAGGER THINKS YOU CLIMB
5.4	5.8
5.5	5.9
5.6	5.10
5.7	5.11
5.8	5.11a
5.9	5.11b
5.10	5.11c
5.10a	5.11d
5.10b	5.12
5.10c	5.12a
5.10d	5.12b
5.11	5.12c
5.11a	5.12d

I always get sandbagged by guys in gear shops. I will stop in somewhere to pick up a cordelette, or a stuff sack, or a guidebook, and they inquire about my plans. Like you do when you work in a gear shop, because that's the good stuff, talking to people about their dreams and climbs and backpacking trips, not which jacket is more waterproof.

But it seems like it always goes like this:

Me: Yeah, we're going to check out [NAME OF CLIMB, GRADE].

Dude in Gear Shop: Oh, that's cool. You know what else you would like, is [NAME OF CLIMB AT LEAST THREE NUMBER GRADES HIGHER].

Me: Uh huh. Is there a good place to get a burrito around here?

Last year, I was in a shop on the east side of the Sierras, talking to a guy, explaining to him that I was going to take my friend from Chicago on his first multipitch climb, so we were going to do something mellow the first day. So the guy in the gear shop recommends a linkup of 12 total pitches ending with the 5.10c Gram Traverse on Drug Dome. Thanks brah, that will be very useful.

I even got sandbagged in a coffee shop a few weeks ago, by a barista. The conversation started out with me asking about her weekend and her asking about mine, and ended with me telling her about One Of The Biggest Days Of My Life In The Mountains and her telling me that she had done the exact same thing this summer, but three hours faster. But then she gave me the locals' discount on my Americano.

I don't know the reasons for sandbagging, psychological, sociological, emotional, whatever—all I know is that it happens. Apparently a lot, at least to me. If you suspect you are being sandbagged, and would like help identifying how, here's my list of four types (probably not at all exhaustive):

1. The Humble Brag Sandbag

An conversation with someone who is a Humble Brag Sandbagger is not about exchanging useful beta—it is about how big that person's [figurative] penis is. As in, You want to know about a good route/trail/ski descent around here? Great. Instead, I shall relate to you how badass of a climber/mountain biker/skier I am.

You: "I was thinking of taking my brother-in-law up Mount Hood next spring, up the standard route."

Sandbagger: "Next spring? You guys should climb Denali. I had the time of my life climbin Denali. What an experience. The thing about Denali is …"

2. The Selective Memory Sandbag

I am not this guy. I struggle and suffer a lot in the outdoors, and am happy to recount every single detail. I do not forget how painful shit is, or scary. I often lead with the number of mosquito bites I got, the slipperiness of the handholds, the density of terrain that must be bushwhacked through. But some people are not like this. They finish climbs or rides or trips and forget every bad moment, and only remember the turns, or the fingerlocks, or the sunset. And that's all they tell you.

ex. "Oh yeah, it was incredible. Kind of a long day, but man."

3. The I-Am-Not-Listening Sandbag

There's no malice here, just someone who is a shitty listener and a bad communicator of useful information. This is the outdoor equivalent of:

"Hey, we are looking for a burger joint. Got any favorite places around here?"

"Do you guys like sushi? You HAVE to go to Izakaya Den."

4. The self-deprecation sandbag.

I have not experienced this type, but a friend clued me into an experience he had had with a mutual acquaintance of ours. Essentially, the sandbagger always characterizes themselves as slow, weak, and out of shape. Then when you get together with said sandbagger, they drop you on a bike ride, or hike way faster than you, or float up the hard pitches of a climb while you desperately grab for gear to pull on. Sometimes this is intentional; they train their asses off but work to create the illusion of mediocrity, and then crush. Sometimes it's not intentional; the sandbagger truly believes they are slow, weak and out of shape—maybe because they compare themselves to Steve House or Anton Krupicka.

Also, FYI, I am not sandbagging you when I say I don't climb that hard. Or run fast, or ride fast. The only time I would sandbag you is when you and I are splitting a pizza, because I assume you can eat as much as me. Which is wrong, and I apologize in advance, but I can't help it. I will eat some of your half if we get the Large.

—

20

YOU DON'T HAVE TO CLIP THAT TO THE OUTSIDE OF YOUR PACK

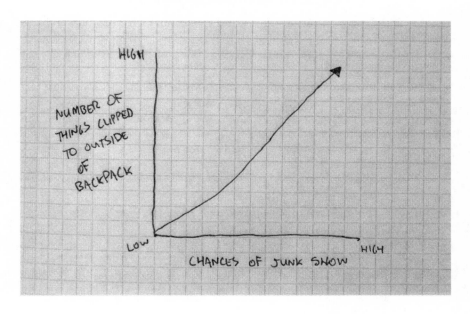

I was renting this guy a backpack and 3-person backpacking tent when I worked at an REI store several years ago, and he and I had the following conversation, as he was holding the tent bag in his hand:

Guy: I bet I could just strap the tent on the back of the backpack here.

Me: You could, but that's about a 7-pound tent, and it's better to have it inside the pack, because the weight will be closer to your back, and you'll have better balance. If it's strapped to the back of the backpack, it pulls the pack away from you. Plus, it can fall off.

Guy: But I could just strap it right here, on the back, right?

Me: Yes, you could, but I'll tell you what I'd do. You're going with a friend, right?

Guy: Yeah.

Me: Take the tent out of the bag and split it up. Give your buddy the rainfly and the poles, and you take the tent body and the stakes. Pack all the solid stuff in your pack, and cram the tent body in last, into all the empty space that's left. Then you have a solidly packed pack, and you can leave that tent bag at home. And you and your buddy are splitting the weight of the tent pretty evenly.

Guy: Yeah, but I could just strap it right here, too, on the back of the pack.

Me: Yeah, you could do that. You could strap it right there, on the back of the pack.

There seems to be this male instinct that the more things we have on the outside of our pack, the cooler we look. Where does this come from? Is there some movie all males watched as young men that taught us this?

We clip coffee mugs, water bottles, multi-tools, anything we can think of, to the outside of our pack, as if that object is so important, we can't waste two seconds opening our pack to get to it. It seems to be a sort of outdoors newbie thing, and then you learn that the more shit you have strapped to the outside of your pack, the more you lose. You learn, then you move on.

Except in the case of one guy my buddy Lee climbed with once. Lee was part of this group of four guys who climbed the North Face route on Longs Peak, a 5.4 rock route in the summer. They had backpacked into the Boulderfield, spent the night, and climbed the route the next day. After they summited and picked up their bivy gear at the Boulderfield, they were re-packing their packs for the 3.5-mile hike down to the Longs Peak Trailhead. Lee was carrying one of the ropes down, and this guy, who shall not be named, sternly said to Lee,

"You make sure that rope is on the outside of your pack when we get to the parking lot."

What does this mean? It means the guy wanted everyone at the trailhead, and in the parking lot, to know that he and his pals had just done an, ooh-aah, technical climbing route on Longs Peak—not like all the other suckers who had just hiked up and done the 3rd-class Keyhole Route. No, this group of men was special. They had used ropes. Like the one that was going to be on the outside of Lee's pack when they strolled off the trail, so they could impress everyone in the parking lot.

Since the day Lee told me this story, we have never failed to include it in every single one of our days out climbing. Just as we are packing up after a climb or a day at the crag, one of us will either clip a No. 3 or No. 4 Camalot to the outside of our pack, or demand that the other guy make sure the rope is on the outside of his pack when we get to the parking lot.

Then we both laugh, crack a couple more jokes about making young women swoon in the presence of all our climbing gear, and we leave.

—

REVIEW: MY RUNNING SHOES

I picked up some sweet-ass shoes after I finally wore out my last pair of trail running shoes after 2 ½ years (the tread was gone and one of the laces finally snapped). There's all sorts of technology and shit in them—there's some plastic stuff on the side, and there are different things to run the laces through, and there's a kind of stretchy thing near the top of the laces. Overall, they're pretty sweet.

I read this book called Born to Run in 2010. You may have heard of it. Author Christopher McDougall investigates the idea that humans are built to run long distances. Among his findings, and you may have heard this, is the idea that we don't need running shoes to be all that fancy. Some people read the book and bought a pair of barefoot running shoes. I read the same book, but took some of the information as a license to just buy old, cheap shoes and fix the way I ran—which could maybe have previously been described as "Clydesdale," but is now more like "gazelle, shuffling in slow motion."

My shoes are circa 2009, I believe—I bought them used at Wilderness Exchange in Denver in 2010 for $40. I believe they are "trail running shoes," although I also wear them on approach hikes to rock climbs, hiking, backpacking, and anything else that doesn't require mountaineering boots. Sometimes I end up downclimbing snow slopes in them. They're not waterproof, but that's OK, because I don't think they were designed to be.

Late last summer, the outer mesh stuff kind of gradually sprung a leak over the course of a 30-mile backpacking trip in the Wind River Range in Wyoming, which ended up being just fine as there was no real structural damage.

Of course, since there was kind of a big hole in the outside, I thought maybe I'd get a new pair of shoes before my pal Greg and I did a one-day Rim-to-Rim run in the Grand Canyon last October. I didn't make time to go shoe shopping, so instead of new shoes, I just brought a couple feet of duct tape in my pack in case something catastrophic happened to them and the sole ripped off or something. They made it fine, but later part of something in the toe section was peeling away and got kind of annoying, so I ended up cutting it off with a scissors.

Based on my research and testing, I believe the ideal use for these shoes is running on trails, or running on other surfaces, or I guess walking too. But also based on my research, you can do basically whatever the hell you want in them. I wore them to hike into a backcountry ski run once, have bicycled up to about five miles at a time, and I think I played my dad in pool once in them too. I also noted that they performed well when I wore them to eat ice cream cones, including this one time I ate two ice cream cones at once because I thought they were really small for $3.50. Essentially, you can count on these shoes.

Or, I guess, you can count on most shoes. I don't really have too many problems with running shoes. I've never been out on a run and said, "Man, I can't go on. These shoes are just not high-quality enough." Usually I get about six or eight miles done, and I'm like, "Man, I'm tired" or "I should call my friend and go smash the breakfast tacos at WaterCourse," or "I better get back to my phone so I can type in this pithy and witty Facebook status that is bouncing around in my head right now." It's really not the shoes that present obstacles to my running.

I have run several 10Ks in these shoes—not 10K races where you register and get a number and stuff; I just like to run for about 60 or so minutes when I go out and I figure that's about six miles or so, which is roughly 10 kilometers. But, you know, these will "go the distance," so to speak, if the distance is like 6 miles. Like if you want to run the Bolder Boulder or something like that. Actually, now that I think of it, I've run about 10 miles in one stretch, too. So go ahead and max them out. I mean, hell, if they can go 10 miles, I imagine they can go 20 or so. I just get bored running that long unless there's food or coffee in the middle somewhere.

Anyway, you should get a pair. Of shoes. Not necessarily these, although I can't complain so far. I think the company that made them in 2009 or whatever still makes them. They're not super-flashy right now, but I noticed if you throw them in the washing machine and get some of the dirt out, they look brighter for a few days.

—

22

THE BEER GRATITUDE SCALE
FOR OUTDOORSFOLK

A while back, I was standing in my neighborhood liquor store trying to decide whether I should buy a bottle of scotch or a six-pack of good beer for a friend of mine. I was borrowing his set of ice tools, and seven ice screws, for a trip to the Ouray Ice Park. My girlfriend does not own ice tools, and I do not yet own any ice screws. And I am big on appreciation. I figure we're talking $400 worth of screws, and $400 worth of ice tools, so he's saving me quite a bit of money by allowing me to postpone my investment.

$11 worth of Dale's Pale Ale ought to cover it. I decided a bottle of scotch would be way over the top.

I was thinking, though, for a guy who doesn't drink, I seem to purchase my fair share of beer, in liquor stores and bars. Maybe it's because in my hometown in Iowa, beer is currency. I bought my first car for $500 and two cases of Busch Light. My father once rented a skid-loader for a day in exchange for eight steaks and four cases of beer. My friend's father once picked up a topper for his pickup truck for $15 and a handle of Black Velvet.

There are certain unspoken levels of appropriate gratitude—you wouldn't ask your friend to help you move furniture all day and buy him/her one drink. No, you would buy them pizza, and a bunch of beer, at minimum. It's the same for the outdoors. I've come up with some rough guidelines to help you decide what's appropriate when thanking someone for an outdoor-related favor.

1 beer:

- Friend/climbing partner picked you up and drove to the trailhead

- You forgot to pack a tire patch kit or extra tube, you got a flat tire, your friend let you borrow their tube/patch

- You borrowed a guidebook

- You ran out of water on a hike and your friend split their last bottle of water with you

- You are very late getting home from hiking/climbing; friend/climbing partner allows you to tell your spouse that it was his/her fault you are late

2 beers:

- Friend/climbing partner picked you up and drove to the trailhead while you slept in the passenger seat

- Friend/climbing partner picked you up and had donuts and/or coffee for you; you did not sleep in the passenger seat on the way to the trailhead

- Climbing partner led the hard pitch, or pitches

- You borrowed a pair of skis or snowboard

- You are very late getting home from hiking/climbing; friend/climbing partner calls your spouse and explains that it was his/her fault you are late

- Friend/climbing partner cooked dinner on overnight trip; it was better than you can cook at home

- Friend brings firewood for weekend car camping trip

- You bail off climbing route, leaving friend's gear (can be more, depending on amount of gear left)

6-pack:

- You borrowed a set of ice tools and a rack of ice screws

- You borrowed sleeping bag, tent, or stove for weekend

- Following a bicycle mechanical on a road ride way outside of town, friend drove and picked up you and your bike and took you home

- You borrowed a friend's mountain bike or road bike

1 beer every time you get together for the rest of your lives:

- Partner dug you out of an avalanche, full burial

- Friend ran to get help when you sustained a leg injury in the backcountry and couldn't walk; you survived

—

THE CARS WITHOUT THAT NEW-CAR SMELL

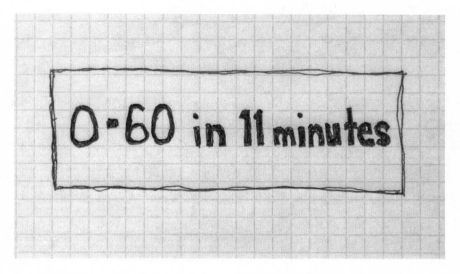

Remember when you first started climbing, or skiing, or mountain biking, and you went out and bought all the gear, and then you immediately sped to a car dealership to purchase a reliable $45,000 sport utility vehicle so you could drive to all places you needed to go?

Me neither. I do remember, in 2006, when someone rammed into my college car, and I got really excited because I was sure it was totaled and I would finally be able to buy an all-wheel-drive station wagon. And I did, for $4,000. Its odometer just turned 220,000 miles a couple weeks ago. It smells kind of like dirt and feet now. One time last fall when I was trying to sleep in the back of it, I started thinking about how its trade-in value was $650, and the box of climbing gear I was spooning was probably twice that.

I always smile at advertising that uses outdoor sports to sell new SUVs, because hardly anyone I've climbed or skied with drives a new SUV, let alone an expensive one. No offense if you do drive an SUV—there are plenty of reasons for buying one. I'm just saying the marketing is interesting when you're, well, essentially the guys and the girls in the ads.

Lots of Americans need a car with the functionality of a minivan, but they want something "sexier." So they get an SUV. The SUV is sexier than a van, because that's what climbers drive, right? It's a sport utility vehicle, and "sport"—mountain sports. Which I guess makes mountain sports sexy.

But most of us outdoorsfolk drive something quite different than a Hummer H3, or BMW X5 or Mercedes G-Class. We drive old pickups with toppers, and then we sleep in the back. We drive old Honda Civics and Subaru wagons with rocket boxes and ski and bike racks on top. Volkswagen vans with stickers covering the bumpers and windows. When the power windows stop working, we help them up by hand instead of spending $300 to fix them—I mean $300, Jesus Christ, that's like half a ski pass, or a new puffy, or five cams. Every windshield of every one of my friends' Colorado vehicles has at least one crack in it. You just don't see too many $60,000 SUVs at trailheads.

I was sitting in my friend's living room talking to him about cars this past fall, and I made some remark about starting a then 2-month road trip in a car that had 200,000 miles on it and no air conditioning. He brought up his old truck, a Toyota pickup with a topper, and said it had broken down on the way back from his 5th wedding anniversary celebration, and he had battled whether or not to fix it or just get rid of it and buy something new. I asked how much the repairs cost, and he said $2,300. I said What did you decide, and he said I just bit the bullet and got it fixed. Ouch, I said, how many miles are on that truck?

330,000.

I thought that was pretty rad.

Brian, another friend of mine who I consider to be a hero/mentor in the ways of living as a dirtbag tumbleweed, once bought a car in Tallahassee for $500. He drove it out to Colorado, then Moab, then all over the place. It went to Telluride Bluegrass. Then he decided he wanted to go teach English in China, so he sold all of his stuff, and the car. Without any mechanical improvements aside from an oil change and some new tires over his 10,000 miles of driving it, he sold it to someone for $950, within hours of posting it on Craigslist.

Brian e-mailed me a photo: "Take a look at that roof rack though. A pair of Yakima bars attached to some some 2×4 blocks with conduit tie-downs, which are then cam-strapped through the door frame. A solid rack though. You could probably lift that fucking car up by it. I am sort of surprised there isn't a commercial design like this—it's 100% universal!"

I bought a minivan a couple weeks ago. I needed something with most of the functionality of an SUV, without the sexiness. So I got an all-wheel-drive Astro Van. I got excited when I discovered it had two cupholders in front, and one perfectly held a Nalgene 1-liter bottle, and the other perfectly held my Pablo's coffee mug. When I told friends I bought a van, a few of them asked, Did you sell your Subaru?

I said No, it's a good car. This past weekend, I pulled it into a storage unit for a little rest, and three of the four zip-ties that have been holding the front license plate in place since 2008 disintegrated as soon as I touched them. The car has no rear defrost, and the rear windshield wiper is stuck pointing toward the sky where it had stopped a couple years ago when the wiring harness melted back there. No cruise control. The molding is missing from the entire right side of the windshield glass, having ripped off on a windy day crossing Nebraska in 2008. There's a slight rattle coming from the gearshift, but if I turn the music up enough, I can't hear it. The air conditioner compressor started slowly dying a couple years ago, just after I had put $1,400 into a new transmission and clutch. Baki, the owner of Roos Only, my auto shop in Denver, had opened the hood, unplugged the wire to the A/C compressor, and said, "There you go. You get some money, you get it fixed."

But I didn't get it fixed. I sweated my way out of Denver last July, starting a five-week road trip that turned into six months, and I put 16,000 miles on that car, drove the entire length of the Pacific Coast, to the

Sawtooths, City of Rocks, the Bitterroots, Tuolumne, the Wind Rivers, Zion, the Grand Canyon. I had some of the best people in the world in the passenger seat of that car, and the only time I wanted to apologize for it was when my friend Greg and I pulled up to the valet at the Wynn Casino in Vegas, you know, sorry it smells like a dude has been living in here. But instead I just handed the lady a $5 tip.

Like I said, it's a good car.

—

DUDE IT'S OK TO HUG YOUR BRO

Get over here. Come on in and let the big bear get his paws on you. Sometimes men are afraid to hug each other, aren't we?

I am not, and I don't think you should be either. If you and I have met before, and interact more than five times a year via any social media avenue or e-mail, I am very likely going to go in for the bro hug next time I see you (instead of a handshake).

If you invite me to stay at your house when I'm in town, or when I'm talking with someone else about you and I say "Isn't that guy awesome?", or you are a generally likeable person whose contact info is in my cell phone, the bro hug is a very real possibility. Unless you want to keep it professional or something like that.

Sometimes, when dudes are happy to see each other but don't really know what the parameters are, they will do that awkward handshake-into-half-hug thing, which is rather unsatisfactory unless that's really what you mean, and usually it's not. It is about as rad as an almost-cold beer or a kind-of-soggy sandwich. It is OK, but lacks authenticity and meaning.

It looks like this: "Oh, are we going to do that ... you know, the handshake thing but ... oh, you're kind of doing the hug with the one arm ... OK ..."

Avoid this. Get comfortable with the hug. This is the 21st century. It's OK. The best strategy to avoid awkwardness is to communicate with proper body language as soon as possible—when you recognize your bro, you open up your arms, signifying Dude, You Are About To Get Hugged.

The proper way to bro hug is to approach your bro with one hand high and the other low—not 10 and 2 in clock positions, but say 7 and 2. That way your bro will be able to come in with his arms in opposite positions.

One pat on the back is the limit here. Two is excusable, but any more than that and you just look like you're really uncomfortable/nervous to be hugging another man in public, which should not be the case.

Don' t—DO NOT—go in for the hug with your arms at the same level, low or high. This forces your bro to take the opposite arm position, and you end up in a very strange hug, one dude's arms up high, the other dude's around his bro's waist, somewhat like junior high dancing (without the nervous armpit sweat and the strange, new tightness in your pants). It also makes it really difficult to avoid your bro's face with your face, and you get dangerously close to kissing each other. Which is of course totally fine, but maybe awkward in a lot of bro/brah relationships.

Other tips:

- Keep an acceptable distance between your crotch and your bro's crotch: at least six inches.

- Duration: A typical bro hug lasts at most three to four seconds. It's OK to have multiple bro hugs, just not all at once. Say you're parting ways after a climbing trip and won't see each other again for a while, so you bro hug, but then you get started talking about some future climb you're going to plan, and then suddenly 10 minutes have gone by since the original bro hug. Then you're like OK, I'm really leaving this time, and you're both going to your respective cars. At this point it is OK to have one more bro hug.

- If you want to add a little more bro-love communication to the hug, like if you're not going to see someone again for a few months, it's acceptable to touch heads mid-hug—but not cheeks.

And, you know, if you see me somewhere, and you need a hug, that's cool. Come on in for it. Remember, 7 and 2.

—

HIKING IS COOL

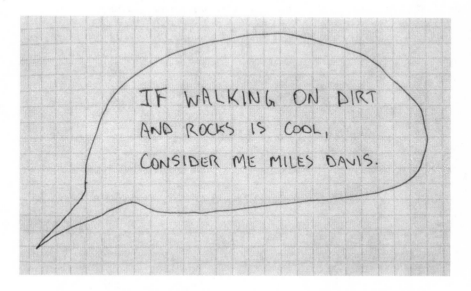

Do you ever think hiking doesn't get much respect anymore?

Wait, better question: Remember that hiking film that showed at the Banff Mountain Film Festival, then went viral after all the magazines shared it on Facebook?

Me neither. But hell, a couple weekends ago, I was out on a trail in Rocky Mountain National Park trying to get a photo of a specific rock formation, and I realized I was hiking. Not mountain biking or approaching a rock climb or ice climb, or skiing or snowboarding, or trail running, or really anything above sub-gnar. But it was ... fun. Fun? Yeah, it was nice.

Fact: Hiking is actually just walking, only on dirt or rocks or other uneven surfaces. Or walking where an animal larger than you can kill and eat you.

Which doesn't get so much love when it has to compete with more XTREME sports in the outdoor realm. Even though you can take your shirt off to do it, and it was basically responsible for Desert Solitaire, lots of Thoreau's material, and all of John Muir's writing, and thusly the Sierra Club.

Also, just FYI, before you get all arrogant about walking to Starbucks to get a latte, remember that hiking was the predecessor to walking. Because there were no sidewalks when your ancestors were out trying to take down a saber-toothed tiger with a spear. They hiked, then later there were roads and sidewalks for walking, and later, there was Starbucks.

Some other facts about hiking:

- Hiking has been known to increase the satisfaction level of many types of freeze dried food, as well as several flavors of energy bars, up to 35 percent.

- Hiking was the inspiration for skiing and snowshoeing. Actually, the rage induced by postholing while hiking was probably the inspiration for those two things, but whatever.

- Hiking often happens spontaneously to mountain bikers.

- Unlike other XTREME sports like rock climbing and heli-skiing, you don't need hundreds or thousands of dollars' worth of gadgets and shiny things to hike. If you have shoes, a Snickers bar, and a bottle of water, you can go hiking. Also, if you only have shoes and no Snickers bar or bottle of water, you can still go hiking.

- If you do want to spend a bunch of money on hiking gadgets, you can totally do that too.

- Bears basically spend their entire lives hiking, and bears are rad.

- You can sometimes see bears while you are hiking, which can be good or bad.

- If you have no idea what the hell you're doing or where to go, there are literally dozens of books about hiking. Try googling "hiking books" and you should find a shitload of them.

- Some hikes end at rock climbing destinations, like El Capitan and Castleton Tower. If you are not a rock climber, hikes that do not end at rock climbing destinations will probably be more interesting.

- Most popular hikes are on trails. You do not necessarily need a trail to go hiking. If you don't have a trail, you are "bushwhacking," which is a lot like hiking, but slower and less fun.

- Hikes range in distance from under 100 feet to thousands of miles. If you have never been hiking before, you should start at the lower end of the scale instead of, say, the Pacific Crest Trail, which requires more skills and sometimes quitting your job.

If you are interested in fun, or nature, or exercise, or breathtaking views, or all four, there's a good chance you might like hiking. Give it a try today!

—

9 REASONS YOU SHOULD NEVER BIKE TO WORK

I find riding a bicycle exhilarating, but that's no reason for you to think you should. In fact, here are nine reasons you shouldn't bike to work. I'm sure you can think of others.

1. It's too dangerous.

Can you imagine being out there on a bicycle with all these crazy drivers flying past you, nothing to protect you except a plastic and styrofoam shell on your head? You could get killed. The absolute best thing is to stay in the protective cage of your car, because no one's ever been killed when they're inside an automobile. Driving is safe.

2. You have to wear a tie to work. Or a suit. Or a skirt.

Not only that, it's important to wear your tie/suit/business casual attire from the moment you leave your house in the morning until the moment you get home. There is no conceivable way you could leave some clothes at your office, and change into them after you ride your bike to work, two or three days a week. Plus, your suit/tie combination is so dialed, you can't just spread your tie collection out over two locations. Where the hell is my cornflower blue tie? I need to see if it looks good with these shoes. And like there's some way to ride a bike in skirt or a dress?

3. You have to go to the gym after/before work.

What, are you supposed to carry all your work materials and your gym clothes in a tiny little backpack on a bike? Please. I mean, what, bike to work, then bike to the gym, then get on the stationary bike for 45 minutes, and bike home? Ridiculous. What are you, Lance Armstrong? I guess you could just ride your real bike, and stop going to the gym, but we're Americans. We work out indoors.

4. You can't show up all sweaty and smelly for your job.

It is a proven fact that once you have sweated from exercise, you can never recover until you get into a shower or bath and rinse it off. Also a fact: Human sweat is comprised of more than 90% fecal particles, which is why you smell like a hog confinement instantly after you start exercising, and afterward, when the people next to you on the stairmaster are passing out like they've just been chloroformed. It's not like you could take a shower at the office, after all, or use Action Wipes to wipe off when you get to work to mitigate that smell. Your co-workers will be all, "Bob, what the hell did you do, bike to work today? It smells like somebody's gutting a week-old deer carcass in your cubicle."

5. You don't have the right bike for it.

The only bike you own are your Trek Madone, and your single-speed 29er, neither of which will work. You'd have to go out and buy a dedicated commuting bike, which start at, what, $1,200? Ask those day laborer guys who bike to work every day on secondhand Huffys and Magnas—they're not cheap.

6. You can't be wearing a bike helmet and messing up your hair before work.

Fact: Hair products are not portable, and are not designed for use outside of your home bathroom or a hair salon. And let's face it: Your hairstyle is a work of carefully crafted art, not something that can be rushed in 5, 10 or even 30 minutes in some modern office restroom. You spend a long time on your hair, just like Tony Manero. You can't just throw it all away on a bike ride.

7. The route from your home to your office would be suicide on a bike.

There are no bike lanes, no shoulders, no wide sidewalks, no nothing on the roads from your home to your office. What, are you supposed to find other roads to ride on, like lesser-traveled, lower-speed-limit roads through residential areas? Or detour way out of your way to get on a bike path? No thank you. You don't have time for that shit.

8. What if it rains?

Yeah, Mr. Hardcore Bike Commuter, what if it rains? You're supposed to just ride a bicycle home from the office through a downpour? What are you supposed to do when you get home, looking like a sewer rat? This is a civilized society. Thanks to umbrellas, sprinting from your car to your office, and sometimes holding a newspaper above your head, you haven't gotten wet outside of your shower since 2007. Next thing, someone's going to tell you that you have to carry a rain jacket in your bike commuting bag—maybe pants too. What the hell is this, a backpacking trip? You're just trying to get to work on time.

9. You would have to change your routine.

Please. Give up your 45-minute drive into work, the drive that energizes you for the day ahead? Give up interacting with all those other fun, friendly, courteous drivers on the freeway? Sitting in traffic? Road construction? Merging? Not a chance.

—

PART 2:

SOME STOKE

MAKE THIS YEAR THE YEAR OF MAXIMUM ENTHUSIASM

One Saturday morning a few Octobers ago, my friend Greg and I were running down the North Kaibab Trail in the Grand Canyon, close to halfway through 26 miles of trail. We had run 4 miles and would run about 4 more to Phantom Ranch, where we could double-fist coffee and Lemmy lemonade at the cantina before climbing 4,400 vertical feet back up the South Rim to finish a hike/run Rim-to-Rim.

I turned around mid-stride and said,

"Hey Greg!"

"Yeah," he said.

"We're running in the Grand Canyon!"

Sometimes I get to do awesome things, and I kind of forget how awesome they are. Do you? I get stressed, caught up in other stuff, and I forget how fortunate I am, how incredible life has turned out to be most days, and some of the special places I've gotten to see. Most of the time, though, I try to keep a pretty good handle on it—try to remember to turn around and yell to my friend that yes, we are running across the most famous hole on Earth, and that's pretty special. Or even reminding someone a few months later about something special.

Kurt Vonnegut, in a 2003 speech to students at the University of Wisconsin, said,

"I urge you to please notice when you are happy, and exclaim or murmur or think at some point, 'If this isn't nice, I don't know what is.'"

This year, I urge you to notice when something is awesome, as it often is, and exclaim or murmur or just make a mental note of it. Isn't it just goddamn fantastic that you have your health, for example? Or running water, or electricity? Or that you have enough money to actually pay someone else to make you a cup of coffee? Or if you want ice cream, you are at any time in America probably only 5 or 10 minutes away from a place that sells some form of it? (Trust me on that one)

Your life, even the bad parts, is fucking amazing. And most of the small things that make up your life are amazing, too—mountain bike rides, rock climbs, ski runs, sunsets, stars, friends, people, girlfriends and boyfriends, dogs, songs, movies, jokes, smiles … hell, even that burrito you ate for lunch today was pretty phenomenal, wasn't it?

What was your enthusiasm for these things last year? I recommend you step it up next year.

People can disagree with things like quality, maybe your taste in food, or whether or not a movie is good. But no one can argue with enthusiasm, especially when it is over the top.

Do you think that climb you just did is the greatest climb ever? Great! If someone tries to tell you it isn't, who cares? "Greatest Rock Climb Ever" is not an objective title. Thusly, when you are excited about a climb (or a trail run or a summit view or a bike ride or a sunrise), don't let anyone bring you down.

A conversation where someone puts down your favorite ski area/mountain/rock climb/trail/burrito is not a conversation about ski areas/mountains/rock climbs/trails/burritos. It is a conversation about that person being a pompous asshole. Go forth and be positive this year.

Enthusiasm doesn't have to stand up to criticism. It doesn't even have to really make sense. If you finish a ski run, MTB trail or sport climbing route, and you love it, I encourage you to try out new superlatives when describing it to someone else. This goes for everything you're excited about.

Examples:

123

- "I'm just going to tell you now that Outer Space is the most incredible rock climb you will ever do. You cannot not smile while climbing it. It's like the Beatles. Even if you for some ridiculous reason don't enjoy it, you can't deny its inherent goodness."

- "Have you heard the new Macklemore song? It will knock you on your ass!"

- "The Eggplant Parmesan sub at Pasquini's is probably my favorite sandwich in the entire city of Denver, if not the state of Colorado. In fact, now that I've said that, I think we should go to Pasquini's immediately."

Maybe some of the stuff you love, that you're passionate about, isn't cool. Hey, this is the 21st Century. Everything is cool. Irony is either everything, or dead. Be honest: When you see someone wearing a Motley Crue t-shirt, you don't know if they're serious, or wearing it to be ironic, do you? Do you like Motley Crue? Then ROCK THAT SHIT. And spread happiness.

Remember it is not illegal to high-five anyone. Do you use exclamation points in the salutations of your e-mails? Well, why not?

Do you like to laugh? Most people do, don't they? Including baristas, waitstaff, and retail personnel. Perhaps you have at some point had a real conversation with one of these people. This can sometimes begin by sincerely asking those people how they are, instead of treating them like a machine that makes you coffee or orders your salad. This opens the door to making them laugh. If you play your cards right, you may be able to high-five them at the end of a conversation.

Remember yesterday, when you saw that one thing that reminded you of that one friend of yours, and you thought about how if you sent that friend a photo of the thing that reminded you of them, they would smile? But then you didn't send your friend that photo, and it wasn't awesome.

Don't do that again. Here's what you do:

1. Take the photo.

2. Send it to your friend.

3. Your friend smiles. The world is a better place. Thanks.

You may have already made some New Year's resolutions, to lose weight, to eat better, to read two books every month, whatever. How about making one more, to be just a little more awesome?

—

28

THE PURE JOY OF FIXIE DAVE

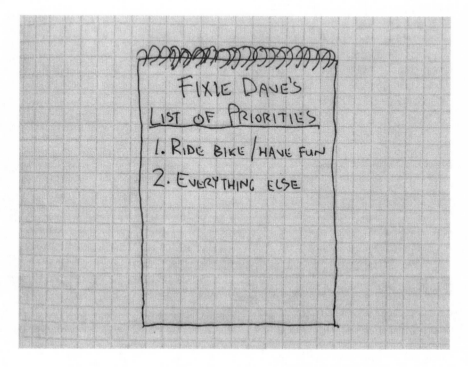

A while back, at a party, I saw Dave Nice for the first time in a long time. We started talking about the interesting nearby town of Colorado City, Arizona, and he mentioned a restaurant there, saying, "I was dating a girl in Kanab for a little while and I would stop there and eat when I rode over to see her."

What is notable about this sentence is that each time he went to see this girl,

(1) Dave bicycled 62 miles each way, and (2) Dave rides a fixed-gear

mountain bike. Dave doesn't drive.

I met Dave back in 2006, sitting outside a coffee shop in Denver. He had the previous weekend ridden the 68-mile Laramie Enduro mountain bike race, and became the first person to ever finish it on a fixed gear. He had also pedaled his bike to the starting line, 130 miles from Denver, over the two days prior to the race.

Dave and I became friends through the weekly Sunday morning breakfast ride at Salvagetti, and I wrote a couple stories about him for different publications—at the time, he was trying to be the first person to finish the Great Divide Mountain Bike Route on a fixie, which some people thought was crazy, some people thought was ballsy, and some people realized was just Dave doing what he did: ride his bike.

I met him at the same coffee shop to interview him for a story for the Mountain Gazette in 2008, and he walked in the door at St. Mark's with a tremendous sunburn. I asked him what he had been up to, and he said he just finished a ride, and listed a half-dozen trails outside of Denver. I asked How long of a ride was that? Dave said about 160 miles. And he was standing next to me ordering a sandwich and a beer like he had just ridden his bike from a few blocks away. I of course asked, Well, what's the longest ride you've ever done in 24 hours?

Uh, 276 miles, over five mountain passes in the Front Range—but that was mostly pavement. Oh, sure, mostly pavement, I said. What did you do afterward? Slept for 16 hours, he said. Of course you did.

Dave loves all the things you love: good food, beer, bikes. He just loves his bike about 1000 times more than you do.

It had been a long time since I'd seen him, but three minutes into our conversation at the party a few weeks ago, I remembered exactly what it was I liked about talking to Dave: Mid-conversation, I am listening to what he's saying, but I can't hear him over the thoughts popping into my head:

I like my bike, too.

I should ride my bike more.

I would be happier if I rode my bike more.

I am going to ride my bike tomorrow.

Where is my bike? Maybe I should just take it on a spin around the block right now.

This, I think, happens to everyone who knows Dave and likes bicycles. Nobody needs to remind him that he loves his bike. It never gets neglected, never gathers dust anywhere. He rode 16,000-plus miles in 2012, went through 11 chains and burned through a dozen tires.

Since Dave doesn't drive, a lot of his miles are commuting miles. He told me once a few years ago—when he was wearing cut-off pants and skateboard shoes—that he doesn't wear lycra when he rides because he wants people to see him riding his bike and believe they can do it, that they don't need to buy a bunch of special gear and clothing to ride a bike. I liked that a lot, because that's the way he is: Not some hyper-ripped athlete, just a dude who wants to talk about good beer and good breakfast joints, and Hey, we should go ride Gooseberry Mesa or Buffalo Creek sometime. And then he goes and rides a century while you're eating dinner, watching TV and going to bed.

Maybe Dave is trying to inspire people a little bit, if you asked him. But I don't think he is. I think he just has a simple, but a tremendous love for the joy that bikes bring most of us, and the courage to make that the central point of his life, not a hobby or an accessory.

I like running into Dave, because he reminds me of the things I want more of in my life, but lose focus of every once in awhile. We always try to remind ourselves, Work to Live, Don't Live to Work, and then we catch ourselves stressing over work again and pushing other things to the side to make room for it. Dave lives to ride, and he doesn't need a sticker on his laptop or water bottle to remind him to do it.

—

THE GUY WHO PUTS THE FUN BACK IN FUN

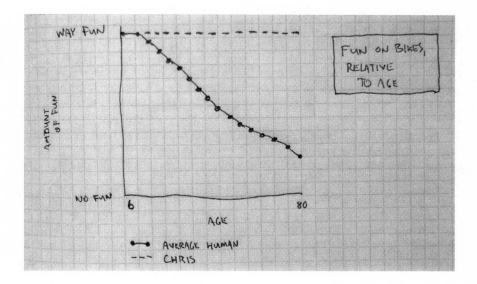

I jogged in my bike shoes with the couple hundred other riders down the dirt road to the start of the 24 Hours In The Old Pueblo, wondering why I'd volunteered to ride the first lap for my team: I still have a cold. Jesus it's hot. There are so many people. Wearing lycra. This isn't my type of thing at all.

Then I saw my friend Chris on the sidelines, sweating in a gorilla suit, minus the head, wearing a Drunk Cyclist jersey.

"Come on," he said, "we're gonna do this Tour de France style." I jumped on my bike and started pedaling, as he ran alongside, pushing with his hand on my back for about 200 feet, giving me an emotional catapult into the race and out of my hesitation. It was his reminder to me: This is not a race. This is supposed to be FUN.

Chris is the driving force behind DrunkCyclist.com, a website that's not so much about being drunk as it is about not taking things so seriously, which is something we've managed to do with a lot of things we do after work for "fun" nowadays. Among all the heart rate monitors, five-paycheck lighter faster better bicycles, maniacal Strava obsessions, and recreational racers using non-recreational dope to get ahead, there is Chris and the guys from DrunkCyclist, who will throw two beers in a backpack for a half-day singletrack ride.

Because we work 40 hours (or 55) a week. The other part of the week should be playing.

We have tons of media offering to help us do things better, faster, harder, achieve our goals, give us a list of 570 tips on how to get stronger, focus our training, cover more terrain, extract the maximum possible amount of something out of whatever it is we used to do for fun. And nobody's writing about going out wandering around on our day off, or accidentally crashing, or daydreaming about the next trip that might not be The Best Ever, but might be pretty goddamn fun if we relax a little bit.

Amidst all the news in my feeds about people crushing climbs around the world, winning races, and pushing physical limits, I find myself clicking on Chris's photos more: he rappelled into a slot canyon with his bike strapped to his back and rode it out. He took a few days off work to try to fatbike the U.S.-Mexico border fence in Arizona. He's in Nepal, exploring trails on his bike, solo. Bikes and beers on Saturday. Bikes and burritos on Monday. Bike ride again on Tuesday. Man, is this guy employed? Yes, he's a chemist.

"I think what makes Chris Chris is that he never has an excuse," his friend Andy says. "People ask how he makes time to do all the rad stuff he does, but in reality, everyone has that time. They just don't have the drive to get out there. They don't have that first kick to get out the door. That's what Chris has, and it speaks volumes for the authenticity of his interest and enjoyment of mountain biking."

Chris does not have fun. He is fun. If he had a spirit animal, it would be a bear riding a perpetual wheelie on a fatbike, high-fiving everyone he rode by. In his words, "I am just a normal guy but I just happen to like being outside by myself a lot. I want to tell my stories and have them get people stoked to go outside." And he does.

I formally interviewed Chris one time, and I asked him the question, "What's one event every cyclist should do once in their life?" I usually expect bicycle enthusiasts to answer, "RAGBRAI," or "Ride Trail X," or "Do Race X." You know, grown-up goals that grown-up bicyclists have on their lists. Of course, Chris said:

"Ride their bike off of a ramp into a large body of water."

30

PLEASE CONTINUE INSTAGRAMMING
YOUR AMAZING LIFE

In April 2013, a piece titled "Stop Instagramming Your Perfect Life" started making its way around Facebook and Twitter. The author raised a point that the things our friends post on social media can make us depressed about our own lives—because we only see people's "post-worthy moments": fabulous meals, vacation photos, good experiences. The title of the piece was later changed to "Instagram's Envy Effect," and it was liked on Facebook 145,000+ times. A quote:

"When you're waiting for your coffee to brew, the majority of your friends probably aren't doing anything any more special. But it only takes one friend at the Eiffel Tower to make you feel like a loser."

I wouldn't be the first person to point out that if you're jealous of your friend's life as it looks on Instagram or Facebook, the problem is not social media—it's you.

My Facebook and Instagram feeds are full of friends getting after it, riding mountain bikes, climbing, catching sunsets and sunrises, dawn patrolling, taking their kids out in the outdoors, capturing their dogs looking adorable—in general, finding beauty in everyday life. Pretty positive stuff, I think. Why would your reaction be to feel bad about yourself when seeing that?

Say your friend Joe Penacoli has just posted another Instagram photo of a before-work ski run, after-work mountain bike ride, or sunset hike. Is your reaction:

a)   "Joe is always doing something cool. I hate that guy!"

b)   double-tapping the photo, causing a heart to pop up on your screen

If you said a), let me ask you this: If you were having coffee with Joe and he was telling you about his recent vacation, would you listen, nod and become jealous of him and think about how you disliked Joe because he made you feel bad that you hadn't taken a vacation recently? Or would you listen and say, "Joe, that sounds really great," and be happy for your friend Joe?

Instagram and Facebook have given us a way to share things instantly, but it should provide more ways for us to be excited for each other, not become more catty and talk shit about our friends. Do you remember life

136

pre-digital sharing? Nobody ever invited you over and said, "Hey, after dinner, I need to show you our photos of the time I got food poisoning and shat my brains out the whole night." Or, "We had a pretty challenging day a couple weeks ago—the kids were being fussy and miserable, crying all through dinner, and Bob and I had a big fight about money. We got most of it on video, want to watch it?"

Are we really comparing our lives to those of our "friends" online? Do we do the same thing in person? Do you hang up the phone after catching up with a friend and say "I hate her. Her life is so perfect."? Well.

I'm a big fan of social media. I like to know when friends find places that make them feel awesome, or do things they're excited to share, or find joy anywhere. I also like photos of dogs, and there appears to be no over-saturation point of dog photos in my social feeds. I know life is hard, and has its ups and downs, and if you want to share those, that's great, too. Please share photos of your new baby, recent trip, day hike, birthday cake, rock climb, sunrise, cute dog, dirty feet, amazing meal, inspiration, and happy moments. I will double-tap that, and click "Like," and I will be happy for you just a tiny digital bit.

—

31

THE IMPORTANCE OF
BEING A LIFELONG BEGINNER

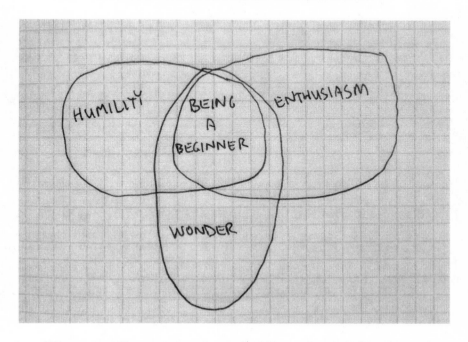

When you dismount a mountain bike going uphill, you end up doing a sort of bow. As you step off and swing a leg over the seat, your head naturally points down as you are admitting that the trail has you beat, this time.

After years of saying "I suck at fast/gravity/downhill sports," I bought a mountain bike a few weeks ago. I have two goals:

1) I will not crash my new mountain bike hard enough to break anything on my body.

2) I will ride my new mountain bike enough times in the next year that its expensive-to-me-but-apparently-relatively-inexpensive-in-the-world-of-mountain-bikes price feels like an investment and not a foolish endeavor.

I'm a climber, I tell myself. I'm no good at these outdoor sports that require fast reactions: tree skiing, mountain biking, kayaking. I'm in my early 30s, too, which is old enough to know I don't have to do shit I don't want to do, like eat cauliflower, get regular haircuts, wait 30 minutes after eating to get back into the swimming pool, or ride knobby-tired bicycles on steep mountain trails. That's the great thing about being an adult.

Which is also the bad thing about being an adult: thinking you know everything. You know what you can do, and therefore you know what you can't do, too. I'm a bad cook. I can't fix a car. It's too late to go back to college. I don't dance. I'm not a mountain biker.

The last word you'd ever use to describe my friend Elizabeth is "arrogant." Three years ago, I would have introduced her as a boulderer, and a good one. Every year since I met her, she's tried something new: Two years ago, she learned to snowboard. Last winter, she learned to tele ski. This year, she says she's going to learn to roll a kayak. I admire this.

I remember learning to snowboard when I was 26, falling on my ass, and my face, repeatedly, cartoon-worthy crashes in the middle of blue runs while 9-year-old kids flew by me carving the hell out of everything as I wondered if I'd just given myself a concussion. I was humbled, to say the least. That year, I was able to tell myself, as Elizabeth does every year when she takes up something new:

I am going to try this, I am going to suck at it for an indefinite amount of time, and other people are going to see me fail, repeatedly.

My friend Jeff Weidman started learning to play the guitar at age 46, and everyone said he was starting too late in life. He stuck with the lessons and kept practicing, as his career brought big changes almost every other year. Nobody said it was too late in life when he played Bob Dylan's "You Ain't Goin' Nowhere" and John Prine's "Christmas in Prison" at his first-ever open mic six years later.

The earlier you can admit you don't know everything, the more time you have to learn new things and make a richer life. The later you admit you don't know everything, the less time you have. And if you don't admit it at all? There's a song lyric that says, "The older I get, the less I know, and the more I dream."

Is anybody inspired by the guy who knows everything? I'd rather talk to the fat guy at the gym who has finally decided to do something instead of slowly dying in front of his TV, the divorcee going on her first first date in 25 years, the shy single guy at the cooking class, all the folks bumbling through our first time in a foreign country and stumbling through a new language, and non-teenagers crashing our new bikes, skis, snowboards, and sheepishly standing up again and believing you can teach an old dog new tricks.

I'm 4-for-4 so far on rides on my new bike without crashing. A couple weeks ago, I swear I caught two inches of air off a small bump in a trail near Fort Collins. If you were standing there and acted quickly, you might have been able to pass a sheet of paper between my tires and the ground. One friend of mine says we peak as bicycle riders at age 13, after which you start to get afraid to jump your bike off things. Another friend says 30 is the new 13.

—

DO YOU HAVE THE STOKE?

2:39 a.m., August 11, 2012: Packs packed, Chris and I are about to shut the tailgate on my van and start walking the Garnet Canyon Trail to try to climb the Grand Teton in one day, one of the biggest, most daunting days I will ever have in the mountains. I tell Chris I have to play one song before we head out, and set my iPhone on the tailgate and push Play on "Theme from The A-Team."

I begin to run in place and spin in circles at full speed in an attempt to make Chris laugh at this ungodly hour of the morning, an alpine start I often like to announce is "so early my dad isn't even out of bed yet." Then I have to stop running because I am laughing too hard at Chris's hyper-speed karate kicks across the parking lot in the darkness.

Three and a half hours later, we are standing at the Lower Saddle between the Grand and the Middle Teton, in the middle of a cloud, and suddenly 40-degree temperatures. We stand there for over an hour, almost ready to head down and give up for the day, or maybe the week, or life. We stand around uneasily, neither of us wanting to call it quits, as if we are mulling over putting down the family dog, and Chris looks up at the Grand and says,

"Let's walk up there and talk about it."

We walk up higher towards the base of the Upper Exum, and 15 minutes later, the clouds begin to break. A couple hours later, we are standing on the summit eating burritos and cracking jokes.

I like to climb with Chris because he is kind of a jovial cartoon character who will not be turned away from a climb by anything less than certainly lethal. It cannot be a chance of bad weather, or high winds—it has to be certain bad weather, or hurricane-force winds. Sixty percent chance of rain? Bah, let's go up there. Raining? It'll let up. Downpour? OK, let's go get coffee and come back tomorrow. He has a kind of permanent positivity, an awareness that any minute he gets outside of the office is a chance to do something rad.

I believe this is an identifiable personality trait called The Stoke. Some people have it. All should aspire to it.

Below is a series of text messages from my friend Josh. They were sent in May and June, not on Christmas Eve. As you can read, Josh is excited about going climbing. So excited, he compares the night before to Christmas Eve. Note his usage of words like "psyched," "pumped," and "WOOOOO."

Excellent. This feels like Christmas Eve.

Partly cloudy, high of 55, occasional wind gusts, i.e., LET'S DO IT! Should I bring anything beyond my rope?

No problemo. I'll pack that stuff & let me know if there's anything else. Psyched!!

So pumped!!!

WOOOOO! I've got a 70m rope and gas/coffee/breakfast money.

Weather looks great for tomw! Psyched!

I like to climb with Josh. Actually, I like to do most things with Josh. He has The Stoke.

The Stoke is usually contagious, and if you are exposed to it and are not infected, you may never develop it.

It is often uncurable. A friend of mine, a few hours after crashing her mountain bike into a tree on a downhill run, summed it up in five words while drinking tequila and hoping to ride the next day:

So painful, so worth it.

The Stoke is my friend Lee driving like a Manhattan cabbie anytime his truck points uphill into the mountains, and leaning forward in the passenger seat when someone else drives, because he is so excited to climb, even after

145

30-plus years in the mountains.

If you develop The Stoke, you will have no shortage of partners in climbing, biking, skiing, or anything else.

People who have The Stoke do not hit the snooze button on their alarm clock and fail to get out of bed to go climbing/biking/hiking/skiing on their days off. They do not complain about food. They do not bail on a day in the outdoors when there's only a 30 to 70 percent chance of rain. In the face of immediate danger, peril, or running out of chocolate, they crack jokes. Statistically, your chances of summiting any climb are increased by 50 percent if you are climbing with someone who has The Stoke. As are your chances of receiving high fives and exploding fist bumps, and in general having an awesome life.

—

THE IMPORTANCE OF BIG DREAMS

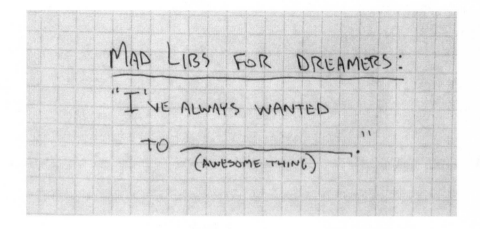

I have a copy of this children's book that I take everywhere I go. It's called An Awesome Book, and everyone I know who's had a baby in the past six months owns a copy, because I bought one for them. It's a kids' book, but I think the message is for adults too.

I like it because it reminds me that I don't need things, but I need dreams, goals, things I decided I wanted to do one day when I was looking out a window somewhere scratching my chin and thinking about what my life should look like. And Dallas Clayton draws incredible unicorns and dinosaurs and bears.

My favorite passage in the book is this:

There are places in the world where people dream up dreams

so simply un-fantastical and practical they seem

to lose all possibility of thinking super things

of dancing wild animals with diamond-coated wings

instead they dream of furniture

of buying a new hat

of owning matching silverware

can you imagine that?

I like to buy books for my friends' children because I think stories are more meaningful than toys, and more memorable. And that goes for adults, too, although sometimes we forget it because we make our lives so hectic.

If you do anything at all in the outdoors, somewhere in your mind is the capacity to dream big, or envision yourself doing something amazing. You want to ride Slickrock, climb El Cap or Mount Rainier, run the NYC Marathon or the Western States 100, or do a raft trip in the Grand Canyon. Maybe you just want to be a climber, or a skier, or a mountain biker. Or marry a beautiful girl, or see the Eiffel Tower, or write a book.

But we get busy. Too busy scrolling our phone screens, watching TV, catching up with all the mundane shit in life and we forget about our dreams. We say things like "I don't have time," and when we get frustrated that we don't have enough time, we assuage that feeling of impotence by buying shit we don't need, which we think will make us feel better. Granite countertops, leather sofas, sometimes skis, climbing gear or bikes we never use. Maybe that's because we're scared of whatever it is we've been thinking about for so long, or maybe it's easier to buy something instead of doing something. Or maybe something we saw told us our dream was something different, and we bought into that.

A few months ago, I was talking to a friend of mine and she told me she had always dreamed of going to Hawaii for her tenth wedding anniversary. I asked Are you going, and she said Well, we don't know, for a number of reasons—a new house, some stress and financial things with a new business, et cetera. I said I think you gotta put that shit on a credit card if you can and go to Hawaii this year. We go into debt for tens and hundreds of thousands of dollars for the most mundane things—houses, cars, sometimes furniture, sprinkler systems—but most of us have a hard time sliding our credit card or taking money out of a savings account to pay for what could be the experience of a lifetime.

If you start a sentence off with, "I've always wanted to …", you either:

aren't going to do it, which means it's not really your dream, or

just haven't done it yet.

Procrastinating, putting it off is fine as long as you're 100 percent sure that you're not going to die in the next year. Because you're going to die someday, and if you're honest with yourself, you will admit that you never once as a kid said to anyone, When I grow up I want matching drapes, or a riding lawnmower that mulches too or a cozy living room. You wanted to be a cowboy or a polar explorer or Amelia Earhart.

—

WHY ROAD TRIPS ARE STILL IMPORTANT

I asked my friend Nick to drive from Denver to Seattle with me a while back, since we hadn't spent several hours alone in a car together since 2008. After 21 hours in the van, I think we got sufficiently caught up. Basically four years later, neither of us have much of anything figured out, especially women, although he must be a little closer because a really great girl is living with him. And it makes me happy that we can spend 21 hours staring out the windshield of an automobile trying to figure things out.

Punctuated, of course, every 17 minutes or so by me saying, "Oh man, this song is fucking amazing" and then turning the stereo up loud enough to rattle unsecured objects off the dashboard.

In a society where you can have almost anything, it's nice to know what you need sometimes. Like really need. The piece that fits in the space that's empty. And a lot of times for me lately, that has been some time rolling down the road at 60 mph or so, watching open country roll by outside the windows. Most of us have a hard time finding places without distraction anywhere anymore. We have TV and computer screens everywhere, smartphones that we whip out of our pockets every time we're unoccupied for more than 25 seconds, and more media to consume than ever. There is hardly anything that holds our attention and focus so much that we will ignore a cell phone vibration or the 200-times-a-day thought, "I wonder if anyone's interacted with me on Facebook/Twitter/Pinterest/ Instagram in the last 6 minutes?"

Except, hopefully, driving. If you're obeying the law in most states, you're not on your cell phone when you're driving, and when you're not in a city and not stopping every five blocks at a stop sign or traffic light, you can just hum along in your car at 60 mph. You have to focus enough on keeping your speed reasonable, keeping your car between the lines, and not hitting anything, but on an open road, most of us don't use that much brain power doing those things. And that leaves your mind to do something our

152

increasingly technology-distracted lives don't allow: Wander.

It hasn't changed in the 50-some years since John Steinbeck wrote about it in Travels With Charley:

"If one has driven a car over many years, as I have, all reactions have become automatic. One does not think about what to do. Nearly all the driving technique is deeply buried in a machine-like unconscious. This being so, a large area of the conscious mind is left free for thinking. And what do people think of when they drive? On short trips perhaps of arrival at a destination or memory of events at the place of departure. But there is left, particularly on very long trips, a large area for daydreaming or even, God help us, for thought. … Driving, I have created turtle traps in my mind, have written long, detailed letters never to be put to paper, much less sent. When the radio was on, music has stimulated memory of times and places, complete with characters and stage sets, memories so exact that every word of dialogue is recreated."

And if you can get some company on a road trip, you might be in one of the last best places to have a conversation with a friend. Men can get together to do things like climb, play pool, hunt, fish, watch sports, drink beer, eat wings—but we have a hard time inviting each other to just go sit somewhere and talk. But in a car, that's what you do. You sit next to each other and find stuff to talk about. Looking out the windshield, there's no football game on, no movie, and no real legitimate excuse not to have an actual conversation.

So you talk about the real shit, life, love, getting older, what you're doing with your lives, what does it mean, what's the point, the things you have space to talk about when you're done catching up with the normal stuff like How's Work, How's Your Lady, What Did You Do Last Weekend, and maybe Who Won The Game or Did You Hear What X Politician Said The Other Day. And I don't know many places where you can make that happen anymore.

If you're not by yourself on a road trip, multiples of two are ideal. Two means catching up with a good friend, four means two people can have a separate conversation in the back seat and you can switch out at gas stops. Three means someone is constantly leaning up to the front seat to try to hear what you're saying, and every time you turn the stereo up, they can't hear anything. And that's a bad deal for everyone, because music is as important to a road trip as gas is. You can spend thousands of dollars on a stereo for your home, theater/surround sound/all that stuff, but the best stereo you will ever own is the one in your car, and its performance peaks when your car is on a road going somewhere other than to your office. It provides a soundtrack to a short movie of part of your life called Let's Go Somewhere And Make Some Memories. And when you're going Somewhere, life tends to be a little more memorable.

—

35

THE MOMENTS BEFORE YOUR BIG MOMENTS

11:41 AM: SWEATING, CURSING,
BATTLING UP TRAIL

11:49 AM: SMILING SELFIE
ON SUMMIT

Last December, I got an email from Statigram offering to collect my "best Instagram moments of the year." I thought Why Not and clicked a couple times, and a few minutes later, I received in my inbox a 15-second video of my five best moments, complete with a piano soundtrack. It was nice. Facebook did something similar and offered to show me my 20 Biggest Moments. That was cool. I scrolled through my Instagram photos and thought, Man, I had a pretty fun year. Scenic, even, if all you saw were the 1-inch by 1-inch photos I posted from my phone.

Memory is a funny thing. As proponents of the "Three Types of Fun" system often point out, your brain has a way of forgetting the bad parts of life, and you only remember the good parts. I didn't post either of those "Year in Review" things to social media, but I did take a look back and try to remember some of the other moments. Things that happened peripherally to all my Instagram climbing and other outdoor shots. The stuff you don't brag about in captions.

For instance: One of the first visceral things I did last year was climb up about 40 feet on an easy route in the Ouray Ice Park and drop a 30-pound block of ice on my right knee, which then bounced off the inside of my left shin and right shin. I tucked my face in between my ice tools and gritted my teeth, waiting for the hammering pain to go away. A few minutes later, I posted a photo of my friend Jesse's wife Melanie toproping her first ice climb ever. Yay!

On April 3, midway through a mountain bike ride near Sedona, I stopped and took a photo of my girlfriend rolling through a meadow in front of Bell Rock as the sun dipped, giving everything a nice golden glow. Fifteen minutes later, I misjudged a step and launched myself over the handlebars, then slammed into the sandstone in slooooooow-mooooooootion OHHHHH FUUUUUUUCK, giving myself a deep thigh bruise and smashing a bone in my wrist. I spent the evening sitting in my van in the parking lot of a supermarket, icing my thigh with a bag of frozen corn. Jealous of my life much?

In early May, I stood on the only spot not covered in pigeon shit in a corner at the base of the east face of Grey Rock at Garden of the Gods to belay my friend Jayson, trying in vain to keep the rope off the literal 150-cubic-foot sea of dried crap covering every surface within 20 feet of the wall.

Later, I posted a quite majestic photo of a climber on the arete to the left, a silhouette high above the valley below, not a clue of the mess of excrement just to the climber's right.

And so it went, throughout the year.

Wow, I remember that sunrise. I also remember the pungent wet-dog smell of my sleeping bag when I unzipped it a few minutes earlier after several days in the backcountry, and I don't own a dog. There's that photo of those two guys climbing on the route next to us. I took that about 45 minutes before we rappelled off the second pitch in a downpour. Sometimes instead of weeping with joy when I reach the belay after a scary pitch, I concentrate on taking a photo of my partner following me.

Don't get me wrong; I had a fun year. I bet you did too, when you look back on it. But be honest: wasn't it also a fun year, fun-in-quotation-marks-fun? Everybody knows that's what makes that sunrise/sunset/summit photo worth it: the cold, the heat, the mosquito bites, the mud on your shoes, the dirt caking your skin, the sand in your eye, the shivering, the bruises, the blood, the sweat, the vomiting—oh, you didn't vomit? Well, trust me, I felt a lot better afterward.

Here's to all the Instagram- and holiday-card-worthy moments—and here's to all the pigeon-shit-infested, accidental bloodletting, dirty, sweaty, morale-crushing times that come before and after them.

—

36

YOUR BEST VACATION IS
SOMEONE'S WORST NIGHTMARE

My friend Aaron is a pretty normal guy, by most standards: High school math teacher, homeowner, happily married, good hygiene, pays his bills, et cetera. We see each other several times a year, and almost every time we get together, we talk about one of his recent vacations with his wife, Krista. Without fail, this happens at least once in the conversation:

1. Aaron tells the story about some part of the trip, which includes one or more of the following: altitude sickness or other illness, monsoon rain, equipment failure, freezing cold, high winds, darkness, constipation, the opposite of constipation, saddle sores, mountain storms, and flesh wounds.

2. I listen, while making a face that is half-smiling, half-cringing, wanting to hear more heinous details, but not wanting to hear more. Sometimes I

interject things like, Oh yeah, that's the worst place for a saddle sore, or Oh, I had that happen with a blue bag one time, too.

3. We shake our heads and laugh.

Aaron doesn't get lost. He doesn't go into things unprepared. But sometimes, when you get halfway around the world, or you're in the wilderness, or on a bike tour, things just happen. These are, as a friend says, the potential side effects of ecstasy. Among all the collateral damage of the vacation, there was a sunset, or a summit, or an opulent meal after hours of near-starvation, or all of those.

I saw a bumper sticker a couple weeks ago that said "My best vacation is your worst nightmare." I was sure I could have a good conversation with the owner of that car.

Pretend you are Bob. Your co-worker asks you how your vacation was. Pick answer #1 or answer #2:

1. Oh, it was great, Larry. I spent Monday through Friday trying to sleep on a thin pad next to two other people in six-foot-wide tent in the snow. We wore three-pound boots with crampons on them, and by the third day, everyone smelled like a dead deer. We walked uphill on hard snow, uneven rocks and ice every day and carried 40-pound backpacks. On the fourth day, the sun came out for a few hours, so we woke up at 1 a.m. and walked uphill at high altitude, and at 11 a.m. we turned around and started walking downhill. Oh, the best part is we pooped in blue plastic bags every day and

carried the bags of poop in our packs the entire time.

2. Oh, it was great, Larry. I sat on the beach and drank mai tais for five days. Got a massage, slept til noon every day. Oh, one day I went snorkeling for a couple hours. It was so relaxing.

Ever notice no one ever uses the word "vacation" when they describe outdoor-centric travel? We substitute "trip." Taking a trip to Yosemite. A trip to Alaska. A trip to Baja. "Vacation" is more like spa, sightsee, relax, recharge, find the perfect balance between sitting and lying down in a chaise lounge somewhere, doze off in the sand—not endo, poop in a bag, get saddle sores, puke from exertion, get gobies from hand-jamming, explore new frontiers in body odor. Isn't it?

I did a fundraising climb on Mt. Shasta a couple years ago with my old high school pal Robb, and he told me that he explained to his dad what we were doing—getting up at midnight, et cetera—and his dad, a sensible man, said: That is the dumbest. Goddamn thing. I have ever heard.

I laughed, because Robb's dad is right. It's absurd what we do for fun sometimes. You could probably say something about the fact that most of us spend 50 weeks a year getting soft behind a desk, and we need visceral experiences to recharge, not more inactivity.

Or you could say people are different—opposites, many times—and in fact, there's a good chance my best vacation is your worst nightmare. Hell, my favorite pizza could be your worst nightmare, and my best mixtape as well. Some of your friends get you, and some don't get you.

Aaron and I disagree on a lot of things, but his definition of fun, and "vacation" is similar to mine, which is maybe why we remain friends after seven years. The first day I met him—actually, the first couple hours—I have this memory of getting my face stung with blowing snow on Flattop Mountain in Rocky Mountain National Park during one of many 40 mph gusts, and Aaron laughing and yelling back to me, "It lets you know you're alive!" Indeed, my friend.

—

37

SOMETIMES YOU GET A HIGH FIVE
FROM THE UNIVERSE

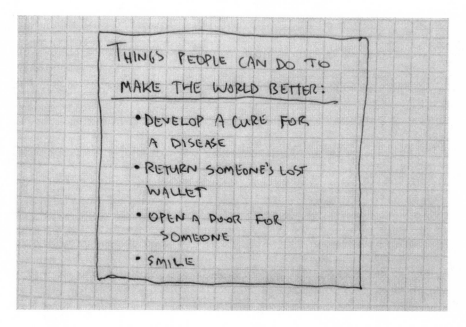

I had about 10 minutes before my flight, enough time to grab one more cup of coffee. I had rushed to finish one more assignment on the floor of the Salt Lake City airport before my flight to O'Hare and somewhat tight connection to Zurich. Just as I was about to order a coffee, I heard a man behind me ask, "Are you Leonard?"

I turned, and a man and his wife stood looking at me, an open passport in his hands. He looked at it, then looked at me, then back at the passport.

"Yes," I said, my mouth dropping. "Wow." I reached out and he handed me the passport, my passport, that I had left on the floor a few

163

hundred yards from the coffee stand. I had hurriedly unplugged my computer from its last North American electrical outlet, packed up my stuff and left my passport, boarding pass inside, sitting next to a potted plant in the busy terminal.

I said Thank You, then Thank You again, and the guy and his wife smiled and walked on their way. I said Thank You 10 more times in my head, stuffed my passport and boarding pass back in my backpack, and ordered a coffee, sighing and shaking my head in disbelief that I left my goddamn passport on the floor of an airport minutes before the start of a three-week work trip.

And that guy saw it, picked it up, and walked around the terminal for a couple minutes trying to find a guy who looked like the guy in the photo, and handed it to me, no questions asked, no expectation of any reward, just doing the right thing on his way to the baggage claim. I did my best to communicate my gratitude, but how do you thank someone for saving you from thousands of dollars in airline tickets, days of stress, missed schedules, maybe identity theft? I should have given him a bear hug right there at the coffee stand.

My friend Mick told me he had a friend who said, "I used to think I was gonna change the world. Now I just let people onto the freeway." I always loved that line, because I think it says something about what people can do to make other people's lives better—all those little things that don't make the

164

evening news.

Most days, I think that most people aren't going to save the world in the way we usually think of that phrase, save the world: feed starving children, rescue families from burning homes, start a nonprofit that helps people find a new start.

But then I think about people like that guy who handed me back my passport, or you, when you find someone's wallet at a restaurant and give it to the manager, or pick up a dropped pacifier for a someone who's holding a baby and trying to juggle three other things, or let someone in front of you in line at the grocery store when they have two items to buy and you have 25, I think Yeah, maybe everyone's going to save the world.

—

38

THE NOT-SO-BAD BAD DAY

Rob at Green Garage in Denver understands the art of telling someone how expensive their car repair is going to be: You can't deliver the news with the same gravitas that you would telling someone they have a terminal illness.

"You ready, man?" he always asks me whenever I take my van in for an oil change. And I brace for the impact on my wallet, which can be anywhere from $250 to $1,500. We go over it, and I shrug my shoulders and say ouch, OK, can you do it today, when can I pick it up, sure thing.

We have such a contentious relationship with vehicles sometimes: we beat the crap out of them, and we feel hurt when parts of them break, even get angry. We accuse manufacturers of building "lemons," or we take it out on repair garages who we think are trying to rob us blind. I try to take everything in stride and not get too worked up about car repairs. I drive a van with 180,000 miles on it, and I put 25,000-plus miles on it each year, I live in it, and its pedigree … well, it ain't a BMW. Whenever I take it in for a checkup, I mentally prepare myself for what I call my "surprise car payment," which sometimes is just an oil change, but sometimes is four figures.

Last fall, I got the bad news that a bunch of repairs needed to be done, costing about what two round-trip flights to Switzerland would cost. It was a particularly large bill, in a year of lots of large car repair bills. I did something I try to never do: I started feeling sorry for myself.

My friend Craig DeMartino has a saying he is fond of: Life is 10% events, and 90% your reaction. This is actually a paraphrase of a longer quote from a book by Charles Swindoll, but I like to think of it coming from Craig, because he's missing the lower part of his leg, has a fused spine, is in chronic pain, and still manages to climb harder than most people with all their limbs.

We sometimes think we have a lot of bad news, but what we often have are small problems plus a huge amount of first-world entitlement. Usually nobody's dying. Most of us don't have to walk two miles every morning to get water from a river. Most of us don't have a huge risk of a suicide bomber stepping onto the bus we take to work every morning. Twitter went down for an hour. The barista obviously didn't get it when we said "extra hot extra foam." Someone pulled out in front of us on our way to work and we had to decelerate 8 miles per hour for almost three seconds.

And then we get angry. Or entitled.

OK, so it's a big car repair bill, or a rejection letter, or a bad this or bad that. But hey, my checking account still has enough money in it for a burrito and an ice cream cone, so it's not that bad, is it? And there's a dog with its tail wagging, and a construction worker telling another construction worker a joke and they're both laughing. And someone out there is having a good day that's far quote-unquote worse than my bad day.

—

39

HOW TO FRIEND SOMEONE IN REAL LIFE

I pulled open the garage door on my storage unit in east Denver, smelling the dust that had accumulated during the two months since I'd last been inside. Jayson had moved out of a 350-square-foot apartment in Capitol Hill and moved all his stuff into my then-half-empty storage unit, filling in the space around my old Subaru wagon.

On the back window of the Subaru, he'd scrawled a note in dust a couple days before he'd left for a six-month stint teaching Bikram yoga in Jakarta:

WELCOME BACK!

HOPE YOU'RE PACKING 4 INDONESIA

7/3/12

LEAVING TODAY

Plus he'd placed a piece of paper under the rear windshield wiper—the paper was 12 years old, pulled out of a printer at an Applebee's restaurant where we worked in college. It had my phone number on it so he could call me and we could go drink beers together and get in trouble, which we did. We both grew up at our own pace, and we don't drink beer together anymore or get in much trouble. We're both address-less, sharing a storage unit, and Jayson's taught yoga on five continents in the past year. The two of us pop in and out of Denver sporadically, the center of our weary universe the guest bedroom at our friend Nick's house near City Park—out of three guys who have been friends since 2000, one of us is thankfully somewhat stable and happy to put up with his two old pals still out wandering around in their 30s.

Sometimes I think I'm lucky to have friends like Nick and Jayson, but I think lucky is the wrong way to say it. I think maybe we just know how to take care of each other. In our triangular friendship, I remember lots of cups of coffee, bowls of pho, checks picked up, car-seat conversations, mountaintops, trail runs, bike rides, and at least two moves of couches up stairwells that would have likely ended less rock-solid relationships. I think Nick doesn't take enough vacations, he probably thinks I'm horribly irresponsible with money, Jayson is appalled at what Nick and I eat, and Nick and I laugh together in wonder at Jayson's next move around the world, wondering if he'll figure it out this year, but not caring if he does.

I e-mail Jayson photos of his mail that comes to my mailbox, Nick only half-jokingly calls the guest bedroom in his house as "Jayson's room," and Jayson and I can't wait until Nick finally gets married so we can co-deliver The Wedding Toast of the Century, which will probably end in a headlock in front of everyone. I'll drop everything to get a cup of coffee with most of my friends, but Nick and Jayson have dibs on one of my kidneys if the need arises. Or my mountain bike.

A couple weeks ago, I saw a headline on the cover of a magazine that read "How To Friend Someone In Real Life." I thought what you probably would think: Wow. Really?

We can blame it on Facebook, or blame it on being too busy, but it's mostly because we're starting to suck at making or being friends anymore, in any real sense. In a generation, we went from little people who made friends based on simple things like riding bikes and baseball cards to big people who are too "busy" to meet someone for lunch if it's not planned out a month in advance, or too shy or lazy to actually ask someone to pick a time and place to hang out.

An old friend told me that in the last years before he quit drinking, he used to see this one guy at the same bar all the time. Every time they talked, the guy would say, "Trevor, you and me, we gotta go fishing sometime." Trevor would say, Yeah, we should go fishing. The next time they saw each other, he would say the same thing: we really gotta go fishing sometime.

But they never went. Trevor told me, "I always wanted to say, 'How about I meet you here again tomorrow night and we'll talk about it again? Because it's never going to happen.'" Neither one of them would commit to getting together outside the bar.

Do we really want to go fishing with each other, or do we just think it would hypothetically be fun if we could ever manage to get around to making plans? Because it's pretty easy. Here's the two-step process:

Hey Bob, do you like drinking coffee/eating restaurant food/rock climbing/mountain biking/something else I like? If yes, then

What are you doing Tuesday after work? Let's go Tuesday.

In a scene in Good Will Hunting, Skyler gives Will her phone number and suggests that they could get together sometime for coffee. Will says, Yeah, or we could get together and eat a bunch of caramels, because when you think about it, it's as arbitrary as drinking coffee.

Which it is. Almost every friend activity is. Drinking beers together, trail running, riding bikes, eating tacos—it doesn't matter what you do, you're just changing the backdrop of a conversation, which is the building block of a friendship. Enough of those, and then you can move on to borrowing money and asking people to help you haul a couch up six flights of stairs.

—

40

MAKE PLANS, NOT RESOLUTIONS

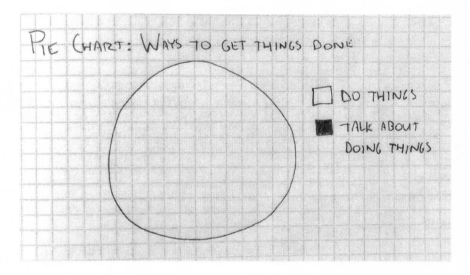

In a scene in the spaghetti western The Good, The Bad and The Ugly, the One-Armed Bounty Hunter finds Tuco Ramirez in a vulnerable position: In a bubble bath. Pointing his gun at Tuco, he begins a speech: He's been looking for Tuco for eight months, and now he's finally got him where he wants him, and … Tuco pulls his gun from beneath the bubbles and shoots the One-Armed Bounty Hunter five times. He stands up in the bathtub and says,

"When you have to shoot, shoot. Don't talk."

Every December, we take stock of what we did last year, writing another chapter in our autobiography. A few days later, sometimes after pounding way too much champagne, we gear up for another trip around the sun by deciding how we want to improve ourselves in the next year. Sometimes we throw out pretty vague statements that don't require us to be accountable to ourselves: I'm going to be a better husband this year. I'm going to lose weight. I'm going to run more.

Every year on his birthday at the end of January, my friend Alan commits to something big for the year. He doesn't hold up a glass of whiskey and announce to his friends that he's going to read 52 books, or go to the gym more often. He puts his money where his mouth is and plans something, with a deposit, or plane tickets. The first year, he called Frank Sanders at Devils Tower Climbing and made an appointment to climb the tower with Frank. Then he went and bought a pair of climbing shoes and a pass to a bouldering gym so he could try to figure out how to climb a little bit before they started up the tower in four months. Another year, he put down a $500 deposit on a Grand Teton climb to raise money for a nonprofit. Next year, the Matterhorn. The next year, a trip to the Bugaboos.

And so on.

Supposedly, if you write down a goal, you're more likely to achieve it. Is that true if you "write it down" in a Facebook status or a tweet?

I don't know, has anyone ever reminded you of something you said on Facebook? "Hey Bob, didn't you say six months ago that you were going to climb more/Mt. Rainier/5.12 this year—how's that going?" Right. Somewhere in a billion viral videos, Oatmeal cartoons, George Takei posts, and vacation photo albums, we forgot about your New Year's resolution.

Did you?

Maybe the question is: Do we really want to do anything, or do we just want to tell people about it?

Business psychologist Peter Shallard says telling people about your next big idea robs you of motivation. You tell people, you reap the rewards of the idea, and then you don't execute.

So are we dreaming, or are we making plans? There's a big difference between broadcasting something about someday riding the Kokopelli Trail and sending one close friend a rough itinerary and asking, What are you doing the weekend of April 20th?

I have a handful of people in my life I share some ideas with, and I am careful which ideas, because there is no lag time between me sharing the idea, and that person asking me "When are we doing this?"

In 2009, The Dirtbag Diaries published an episode called The Year of Big Ideas. Fitz interviewed Rangi Smart, a high school math teacher who found a 20-foot constructed jump on one of his favorite mountain bike trails and decided he was going to take a shot at it. He told his wife, then a few friends, and no one shared his stoke. You're an adult, they said, you're providing for a family, et cetera. So he finally told the only people he knew would hold him accountable, to back up his talk: His 9th- and 10th-grade students.

"Once I told my classes—I got 160 students—and I started making verbal commitments to them," Rangi said, "Then it was over. I had to do it."

Rangi told his students because he wanted them to make him feel like he had to hit the jump, not because he wanted them to think he was a rad mountain biker. Then he went out on his own and stuck the landing—barely.

Me, I got a few plans for this year. What are they? Hey, if you have to shoot, shoot.

—

ABOUT THE AUTHOR

Brendan Leonard is the creator of Semi-Rad.com, and a contributing editor at *Adventure Journal*, *Climbing*, and *The Dirtbag Diaries*. He grew up in Iowa, moved to Montana when he was 23, and realized he'd probably never move away from the mountains after that. He has climbed, backpacked, and mountain biked all over the West, and his stories have appeared in *Backpacker*, *National Geographic Adventure*, *Outside*, *Men's Journal*, *Sierra*, *Adventure Cyclist*, and in his first book, *The New American Road Trip Mixtape*, published in 2013. His favorite place to write is still Semi-Rad.com. He lives in Denver sometimes, and sometimes out of a van rolling around the West.